The Finisher

A New Path for Your Second Half

By Jan Kinne Conway

Jennys
Go for it
Follow your dream!
Blessings
Jan
Acts. 20:24

IPG

Intermedia Publishing Group

The Finisher

Published by:
Intermedia Publishing Group, Inc.
PO Box 2825
Peoria, AZ 85380
www.intermediapub.com

ISBN 978-1-935529-10-1

Printed in the United States of America by Epic Print Solutions

Endorsements

The Finisher is a story which speaks to the desire of every Christian heart. With insight and humor, Jan Kinne Conway captures the spiritual strength of a great man who ran his race with the goal of finishing well for God's glory. This is a story to read and treasure and pass along to everyone you know.

Bodie Thoene,
Best selling author, 45 books of Christian historical fiction

Some books make you a better person, just for reading them. *The Finisher* is such a book. Jan Conway has captured a life well lived and inspires us to do the same. If you are at a fork in the road in life, no matter your age, *The Finisher* will challenge you to take the risks, believe God, and go after the full abundant life God promises. If you are tired of the ho-hum of life, or if the stress of life has gotten you down, pick up this book to pick up your life. Be careful, it comes with a warning: **Read at your own risk—your life will never be the same!**

Bill and Pam Farrel
International speakers, authors, 28 books such as
Men Are Like Waffles, Women Are Like Spaghetti

This book is about an extraordinary man, an amazing adventure, and – most of all – divine purpose. Jesus calls us to produce "fruits that last," fruit with eternal significance. This book will inspire you to focus on what really counts as you finish your one, and only, life.

Kent Hunter
Leader, Church Doctor Ministries

Doug Kinne is an inspiration to others who want the second half of life to be more fulfilling. He walked away from a comfortable life style in midlife, and used his profession to make a difference for eternity. You will be inspired by his life and challenged to consider a change for your life.

Loren Cunningham
Founder, Youth With A Mission
President, University of the Nations, Kona, Hawaii

Reading this book is dangerous. You will be profoundly moved to action! *The Finisher* is a warm, touching, funny, yet practical book with specific help for the second half of your life. Jan writes from real life – she has been where you are! She is authentic, vulnerable, and radiates enthusiasm! She gives practical steps so that your life can "Make a Difference".

Jim Conway, Ph.D.
President, Midlife Dimensions
Author, 16 books such as *Men in Midlife Crisis, Traits of a Lasting Marriage, When a Mate Wants Out* and *Women in Midlife Crisis*

I often recite the story of Doug and Jan Kinne. Had Doug waited until the conventional time to retire, he would have missed it. This is the story of an early finisher, a partner in the gospel, and a friend who is now part of the great cloud of witnesses. I pray it challenges you to consider your second half and the legacy you want to send ahead.

Nelson Malwitz
Founder and Chief Innovative Office, Finishers Project

Foreword

I first met Doug and Jan Kinne in 1992 when they came to the University of the Nations in Kona, Hawaii, to staff a health care school.

Doug had left his OB/GYN medical practice at the age of 49, had a passion for the lost, and a vision to train other medical professionals for missions. Following their training, Doug and Jan joined us in Kona on the Crossroads Disciple Training School staff and developed a special medical crossroads curriculum. In 1997, Doug was installed as Dean of the "College of Counseling and Health Care" at the Kona campus. While Dean of the College, Doug developed the HIV/AIDS course, and co-authored the Introduction to Children's Social Services course.

He loved people. Doug was equally comfortable with leaders of nations as well as the homeless. He died in 2000, at the age of 58, yet his legacy continues on through the students he trained and the courses he authored. Medical clinics, orphanages, and churches exist today because Doug answered the call of God. He finished the task given him to do.

Jan's passion is that you the reader will not wait until it is convenient to follow the calling of God. I pray after reading his story, you will know God more deeply and make Him known to others - while you still have the time.

Loren Cunningham
Founder, Youth With a Mission

Dedication

To my father,

Harry Becker, Doug's best friend,

and

To our children,

Rex, Matthew and Tamara

Acknowledgements

This book has been a work of the Holy Spirit. When I first felt impressed to write Doug's story, I thought God must be kidding. Who me? I'm a nurse not an English major.

I was at the University of the Nations in Kona, HI. They have an excellent writers group led by Sandi Tompkins. I joined. They lovingly embraced me and my writing project. The first time I read in the group, one of the men cried. It wasn't my writing, - it was horrible. It was the message. I knew then, I must continue to write this story. They helped me become a writer, encouraging and cheering me to continue when I felt like," what's the use." I cannot say enough good things about this fantastic group of people. I love you all very much. Thanks for being my cheerleaders!

I took the Authors Training School at the university led by Betty Barnett and Sandi Tompkins. Thanks to all the staff and students in that 2002 school. I received "the most improved" award at graduation! Mahalo staff!

Elaine Colvin Wright taught in my Authors Training School. She saw in me what I didn't know was there. She took me to my first writer's conference and made sure I connected with the correct workshops and people. You're a blessing Elaine

Barb Overguaard spent time at my home in Michigan and did the first edit. Sandi Tompkins did another edit after I made improvements. Many friends have read the manuscript such as Tod Kingsland, and made needed suggestions and corrections.

Many thanks to the students and staff in all the various classes we taught, some of whose influences are written in this story. I also want to thank my family and friends who told me to never give up

To Nelson Malwitz, Founder of The Finishers Project. He called Doug his "poster child". He showed me through this organization, that others in Midlife want to make a difference, but some just don't know where to start (See web resources back of book).

To Brad Benbow, who never met Doug, but changed his life focus after hearing Doug's story. He is an encouragement to me, that others who read this story might do the same.

Finally, to my husband, Jim Conway, who wouldn't let this book die in my computer. He prodded me to "get it out there" to help others. Our prayer is that you will be blessed by reading Doug's story, and that it will encourage you. Don't wait - make a difference!

Jan Kinne Conway
Crooked Lake, MI
2009

Table of Contents

Introduction ix

Chapter 1 A Hectic Path:
                   Life is too Busy 1

Chapter 2 A New Path:
                   Trying out a Different Lifestyle 15

Chapter 3 Early Life Path: *Birth, School,*
                   Marriage, Family 35

Chapter 4 Preparing for a New Life Path:
                   Skill Development 49

Chapter 5 Uncharted Path:
                   Opening a Closed Country 73

Chapter 6 Traveling our New Path:
                   Comfortable in Our Calling 89

Chapter 7 Rocks in the Path:
                   Our Greatest Challenge 109

Chapter 8 The Upward Path: *To the Courts*
                   of the Living God 127

Chapter 9 My Path: *How will I Finish?* 141

Chapter 10 **Changed Lives from Changed Paths**
The Ripple Effect - Lasting Fruit.....**151**

Study Guide **165**

Resources **181**

Introduction

This book has been written in response to the many questions I receive almost daily – questions about how we changed careers and went into full-time missionary work at midlife. My husband and I quit our jobs in the medical field when we were in our late forties to go into missions. People frequently say, "I would love to do something like that, but I can't see how I could." They usually go on to tell me the kids are in college, they have aging parents, a mortgage on the house, the list goes on, unique to each person, yet strikingly similar. "Tell me how you did it," they ask. When I start to explain, I usually hear, "Well, I can't even consider this right now, maybe someday...!"

Well, I'm here to tell you that "someday" may never come. I encourage you, if you feel God leading you to do something different with the rest of your life, don't wait! You might not have the time left you think!

On October 14, 2000 at 1:06 a.m., I took my husband Doug's hand and handed him over to Jesus! At that moment when Jesus took him home, Doug finished his race.

Doug's story, along with others whose lives have made a difference, could be a model for you and give you idea's of how to walk on a new path with purpose. These examples are meant to encourage you – first to get unto His path, then to run your race well, and finally to stay until you reach the finish line.

When my 58-year-old husband died, a scripture verse from Acts 24 came to mind, *"If only I may finish the race and complete the task the Lord Jesus has given me to do" (NIV).*

Doug finished the task given him to do. What an honor it must have been for him to reach heaven and hear our loving Father say, "Well done, good and faithful servant!"

When Jesus died on the cross, He said, "It is finished." God places a high value on *finishing!*

Are you asking the question, "How can I make the rest of my life count more than it already has for God's Kingdom purposes?" If so, in the back of the book is a Study Guide section you might find helpful. It can be used individually, with your spouse, or with a small discussion group. You will find "Points to Ponder," "Practical Steps to Proceed," and a "Prayer for Pruning."

In Chapter 10 are a few short stories about others I'm acquainted with, who have also left careers to do mission work, people who literally took the plunge.

Finally, I pray you will be blessed in hearing an update about those who were the fruit of our decision to change direction. I pray this book will cause you to re-evaluate your life and its direction. If you are contemplating a change, I hope it will encourage you to follow your dream, run your race, and complete the task given you to do, while you still have the time!

The Finisher

"It's amazing how a simple man,

Can influence so many people,

In so many countries around the world."

Sasha Volyanyk,
Director, YWAM Ternopil
Ternopil, Ukraine

Chapter 1

A HECTIC PATH:
Life is Too Busy

"I feel like I'm in a revolving door, and I don't know how to get out."

Doug Kinne, 1986

The smell of coffee brewing filled the house. Lacking was that comfortable warm feeling I usually associate with my favorite morning aroma. Today there would be no comfort; after a long illness, my husband Doug had died during the night.

I was numb. He had been ill with a brain tumor for the past eight and a half months, but his death was still a shock just beginning to sink in. My husband, my best friend, was gone. *Why Lord, why? He was in the prime of life,* "*Midlife.*" *He was doing so much good for You. He had so much left he still wanted to do. Why?* Heaven was silent.

I curled up in my favorite chair with a cup of coffee nearby. My morning devotional led me to Acts 20:24. "*However, I consider my life worth nothing to me, if only I may finish the race and complete the task the Lord Jesus has given me . . . .*"

Heaven softly answered my heartfelt question: Why Lord? "*He finished the task given him to do.*"

So that's why. In the midst of the numbness, I was starting to understand. I pondered, *what if Doug had not taken a long hard look at where his life was going?* He didn't have the time left to live that he thought. But, he had made some choices and took intentional steps years ago which allowed him to finish his task.

Long ago God had planted a seed in our hearts concerning medical missions. Years later He took that seed, and after it had been watered, it grew. It became a strong desire in our hearts. God took that desire and drew us into His plans and purposes for us in a fresh new way. As I look back, I now see how God directed us to "a new path in our second half."

Is This All There Is?

A caged rat runs on a wheel getting nowhere. *Nowhere,*

that was once where we seemed to be going. *When did life get so out of control?* Something or someone always screamed for our attention, and now email. The list seemed endless. Even scheduling our recreation had become frantic. With all our modern conveniences, we should have had more time for what really matters: spouse, kids, church, and friends. However, we had less. Life got out of control, and we didn't see it coming. Life felt like one big rat race.

The Race Is On!

We were a typical American family. Too busy! The rat race seemed to be intensifying. It shouldn't have been. Our children were mostly out of the nest. But that year, 1986, they were all home for the Christmas holidays. Rex, our oldest, was twenty-two and in his last year of college. Nineteen-year-old Matt was a college freshman. Tamara was sixteen, a freshman in the Christian high school. I worked part-time as a Registered Nurse at the hospital.

Life was going on as usual, and once again, as many times before, I felt totally frustrated with our situation! I was trying to manage my household for Doug and the kids. The roast I prepared with such love was drying out in the oven. *Would it always be like this?* Being married to a busy Obstetrician/Gynecologist physician was taking its toll on all of us, not just the roast in the oven.

I heard the garage door open and immediately Doug's beloved English Setter hunting dog, Holly, ran to the door, jumping and barking out her greeting. *How I wish I could match her unconditional enthusiasm!* I could only think about the dry roast and the fact that he hadn't called to say he'd be late for dinner.

Doug trudged through the door, looking tired after another busy day at the clinic. "Hi, I'm home. What's for dinner? Where's the mail?"

In the early years of our marriage, when Doug was attending medical school and completing his residency at the University of Michigan in OB/GYN, I had been more supportive. We were a team with one goal, getting him through school. If he needed to stay late for emergency surgery or just to complete his long list of clinical patients, I had understood. But now, since he was a practicing physician, it seemed to me that he should have more control over his own schedule. My emotions now reflected the strain of the years, and I too had grown weary of our lifestyle.

"Doug, you're late. The kids and I have been waiting for you for half an hour and the roast is overdone! Did you break a finger?" (This was our code for, "You could have at least called!")

"Yeah, I know, I know. Just give me 10 minutes to unwind and look at the mail."

"Well, all right. You know that you have an elders meeting at 7:00 and it's already 6:30. You could have at least called..."

"*Please*, can you just give me 10 minutes to myself?" I saw the pleading puppy-dog look in his eye and knew I'd better give him 10 minutes.

Doug walked into the living room carrying the mail. Matt looked up from the sofa where he sat reading, "Hi, Dad. How's it going?"

"Fine," Doug mumbled wearily, flopping himself down in the chair next to the Christmas tree.

As he sorted through the mail, Rex bounded up from downstairs where the boys each had a bedroom off the family room. "Hi, Dad! Hey, want to go snowmobiling tomorrow?"

Tami, hearing her dad's voice, made her way into the living room. She was no longer into doing stuff with Dad. She had a busy life of her own, filled with cheerleading, snowmobiling, skiing and riding her horse when it wasn't winter. But she sure liked to talk about what she was doing! Doug had no energy to even acknowledge her. His face was in the mail.

I called the kids into the kitchen. "Please, guys, just give your dad a few minutes to read the mail. Rex, finish setting the table. Matt, here's the silverware. Tami, the napkins need folding." I hoped to keep them busy to allow Doug some time alone. We all just hung out by the kitchen counter and chatted. It was nice to have them all in the house again. We always had lots to talk about when we were together. Ten minutes ticked by quickly.

I called everyone to dinner. "Sit down, guys. It's time to eat. Your dad has a meeting!"

"You're leaving, Dad?" Matt asked plaintively from the kitchen. "We haven't seen you in two days. You were on call last night, and I was hoping. . ." his voice trailed off. By this age, he had gotten used to his Dad rushing off to a meeting or to deliver a baby, but the sting of disappointment was still there.

As I walked into the living room, I caught the look of resignation in Doug's eyes. He couldn't be three people at once, he was only one. He shrugged his shoulders, left two days worth of mail beside his chair, and came to the table for dinner.

We were once again together as a family for a meal. My mother's heart smiled, in spite of the overdone roast. After saying grace, we all added our "Amens."

Doug sighed, "It's great to be home. It's been a long couple of days. How is everyone?" Before anyone could answer he added, "Maybe tomorrow night we can catch up."

I hated being the bearer of bad news. "You're on call

again tomorrow. Remember, you agreed to cover for Dan?"

"Oh, yeah, well, maybe if I'm lucky no one will need me." Doug turned to Tami and smiled. "I'll tell you what. You pray that nobody goes into labor so I can stay home. He shuffled in his chair, and his voice trailed off, "Yeah, maybe tomorrow night then."

Tami smiled back at him and Rex quickly interjected, "Don't forget, Dad. We need to get out on our snowmobiles!" Matt chimed in with a reminder of his own. "We're going to a movie Friday night, aren't we, Dad?"

A loud "r-r-r-i-n-g" interrupted our limited family time. "Rex, answer that, would you?"

Sitting next to the phone, he reached over to pick up the receiver. "Hello . . . Oh, hi, Pastor Bill . . . Sure, just a minute, I'll ask him." Rex lowered the phone.

"Dad, it's Pastor Bill. He wants to know if you're coming to the elders' meeting tonight."

Doug waved his fork in the air as he spoke with his mouth full. "Tell him I'm on my way. I just need to finish my dinner."

Rex lifted the phone back to his ear. "Oh, you heard him, huh? Okay, bye." He hung up the phone.

"Dad, he said to finish your dinner because if Mama ain't happy, ain't nobody happy and she wouldn't be happy if you didn't eat everything she cooked for you!" Everyone smiled a knowing look.

Doug gulped down the remainder of his dinner and rose from the table. "I'll see you all later! If you're in bed when I get home, I'll see ya tomorrow."

He left the room to a chorus of voices. "Bye, Dad. See ya later, Dad. We love you, Dad." *I wonder if he remembered the unopened mail left on the table as he walked out the door.*

Once again, I was left at home with the kids, desperately trying to direct traffic and fill the vacuum in their hearts left behind by their absentee father.

"Matt, it's your turn to clear the table. The rest of you can go do whatever." I stayed to help clean up the kitchen. My heart was as cluttered as the table, full of the leftovers of Doug's time. If only I could clean up the mess our busyness had created, as easily as I could clean up the table.

Matt stood in the kitchen with his hands full of dirty dishes. "Mom, why does Dad have to be gone all the time?"

Although I felt frustrated with the situation myself, I quickly rose to Doug's defense. "Your dad has a lot of responsibilities, Matt. He has an important job as a doctor and never knows when a woman will go into labor. He has to take his turn on call every three days." I started listing other activities on my fingers. "Then there are the School Board meetings every week and elders' meetings, like tonight, besides Medical Society meetings, and then he's president of the Ruffled Grouse Society, and of course we go to church on Wednesday night..."

Matt interrupted my recitation. "Mom, I wish . . . I just wish . . . I go back to college on Sunday."

I nodded and put my hand on his shoulder. "I know." Then I brightened. "Just think of all the nice things we get to enjoy because Dad has such a good job. We live in a big house, and you got your new ski equipment for Christmas, remember? Plus a season ski pass! Lots of families can't afford all that. Even if they do, very few have new Rossignol skis!"

"I know, Mom, but you can't talk to skis."

I turned back to Matt. "Give your Mom a hug!" He walked into my waiting arms. *Maybe one day life will slow down,* I thought. "You know Dad loves you and wishes he could be with us more. Maybe some day..."

"Sure," Matt said lamely, "maybe some day. . ."

Could There Be Something More?

"Hon, I'm home!" It was after 11:00 p.m. The dog didn't bother to greet him this time; she settled for thumping her tail several times on the carpet. All three children were either still out or in bed when Doug finally returned from his elders' meeting. He looked as tired as the dog, but he was still standing!

I had waited up for him. I was sitting by the fire reading when he walked into the living room. Being a full foot shorter, I stretched my neck and stood on my tiptoes to reach his 6' 4" frame. This time I greeted him with a kiss. "Did you have a good meeting?"

"I guess so," he said. "But it's just so aggravating. We spend so much time and energy splitting hairs over dumb stuff. If people would only use more wisdom, we wouldn't need half of these meetings!"

I nodded. "Would you like something to drink, honey?"

"Yeah," he said, "something without caffeine. I really need to sleep. I just want to relax a minute first." Then, he looked deep into my eyes. "Jan, can we talk?"

"You want to talk?" I quipped. "I don't believe it!"

"Don't get cute, woman," he said with a twinkle in his eye. "Just get me something to drink and have a seat."

"Let's sit by the fire," I suggested.

"Okay, as long as it doesn't put me to sleep. I'm so darned tired! I was up all last night, delivered three babies, and then had an office full of patients all day."

I came back with our drinks and settled in next to him. I

loved our fireside chats. We had been married for twenty-three years. At first, we seemed to talk frequently. When the kids came along, there seemed to be less time for such intimacy for just the two of us. Most of our conversation was spent discussing the kids or household issues. It had gotten down to about three or four times a year that Doug really felt like baring his soul. I had a feeling this could be one of them.

His face grew serious. "Jan, I don't know how much longer I can keep this up. You saw the disappointment in the kids' faces tonight. I have no time. It seems I have no time for anything except work and meetings." A cloud of grief passed across his face. I nodded with understanding – and complete agreement.

Doug continued, "I feel like I'm stuck in a revolving door. When I walk out of one room, my nurse sends me into another. When I walk into the house, you send me back out to my next meeting. I feel like a robot responding to a control button in the hands of others. You know, I could drop dead from exhaustion tomorrow, and they would find someone else to deliver babies. The clinic would go on as usual. Why am I doing this? Why am I working so darn hard? For what? I feel like I'm on a treadmill, running as fast as I can but getting nowhere. Jan, I'm so tired. There must be something more." He slumped into me, and I held him for a time. What was there to say?

Slowly, a thought took shape in my mind. I could see

us in a rustic setting, living in a far-off land where the pace of life was much slower, yet somehow more meaningful. I turned to Doug, almost afraid to verbalize what I saw.

"Doug, do you remember when we were dating, and I told you that I wanted to be a medical missionary? You said that you'd like the same thing some day, too. Remember that?"

"Yeah, I do, but I don't see how we could be missionaries any time in the near future. The boys are still in college and Tami is at Harbor Light School. They're all expensive. That's a lot of tuition to pay every month, and we have other expenses too you know – house, cabin, cars . . . ." His voice trailed off, his mind lost deep in thought.

I felt my insides sag, "I suppose you're right. But it was such a lovely picture."

We sat in silence for a few moments, pondering the fast-paced life we had created for ourselves. *Could this really be life as God intended it to be lived?* I thought.

Suddenly, Doug turned and looked deep into my eyes. "Jannie!" *Was that hope I heard in his voice?* "Do you see any way we could go on a mission trip now?"

My spirit leapt. "Doug, let's ask Pastor Bill if he knows of someplace that we might go for just a short time. It would do you good just to get away."

"I do have a month's sabbatical coming," excitement

was now growing in his voice. "Maybe I could take it and go to a country where I could teach… I wonder if they need that kind of help anywhere in the world?"

"Maybe, just maybe I could teach CPR," I added. "I bet they don't have that in developing nations."

"Doug," I continued with a new level of enthusiasm, "I think if God wants us to go. He will make a way. Something will just fall into place for us."

"Let's try. You make the call. Let's just see what happens."

For the first time in months, I sensed a hint of hope in his voice. We sat staring into the fire for a while, each lost in our own thoughts. Then it was time to go to bed …time to dream.

Chapter 2

A NEW PATH:

Trying Out a Different Lifestyle

"...first sit down and estimate the cost..." (Luke 14:28).

Testing the Waters

"Go on a short-term mission's trip," we were told. "It will change your life." We would soon find out if that were true. After our conversation by the fire, we began to search out the possibilities. Pastor Bill put us in contact with a missionary from our church, Terry Bennett who was in Haiti. Terry would have loved to have us come to Haiti, but felt it wasn't safe because of a pending revolution. Terry made some phone calls of inquiry; one was to Judge Patterson, the Supreme Court Justice of Grenada. No, they did not need help at the medical school in Grenada, but a phone call to his former law school classmate, now the President of Guyana, provided the answer. They desperately needed help and good teaching at the medical school in Guyana. If we would consider coming to help teach, he would see that we got the necessary invitations and visas.

Guyana is an English-speaking country in South America. It was British Guinea before becoming independent in 1966 from the United Kingdom. Some people say it was now a socialist government with Communist leanings. Once Guyana gained its independence, their infrastructures began to deteriorate.

In 1978 almost ten years before our arrival, a cult leader from the USA, Rev. Jim Jones had taken his followers, members of The People's Temple, from California to Guyana and set up a colony in its jungles known as Jonestown. Jim brainwashed his followers and forced them (either voluntarily or involuntarily) to drink poisoned Kool-Aid, resulting in the deaths of 913 people on Nov. 18, 1978. He then took his own life.

The government was (rightly so) suspicious of Americans. Since that tragedy, we were told they were not issuing visas to Americans. However, Terry arranged through Judge Patterson, who was Guyanese, to get us visas. He also wanted to go with us. He would teach us how to share the gospel while doing our medical work. Since this all sounded rather scary, we were more than happy to have a seasoned missionary accompany us!

In the midst of getting ready for this new venture, I still had to get used to the idea of going on a missions trip. I wondered, *"Is this the elusive something more we are seeking, or maybe at least a doorway to it? Could this really be the answer?"* I was excited at the prospect of a new direction for our lives, but, on the other hand, I still couldn't imagine what it would be like. I was used to things being pretty nice. I wondered, *"How would I handle the change, even for a month?"*

Visions of potential scenarios filled my mind. I am not a camper. My idea of roughing it is going to the Holiday Inn without a hair dryer. Doug, on the other hand, was a deer hunter. Going days without a shower was no big deal to him. I wasn't so sure that if I went on a short-term mission trip I'd ever want to leave my nice house again! *Women need security*, I reminded myself. On the other hand, I reasoned, *I've always wanted to be a missionary.* A short-term trip would certainly be a way to test the waters.

I remembered once telling my kids, "You can stand anything for a short period of time." Now it would be my turn to "walk the talk." After all, it was just a month, not a lifelong commitment. Better to find out now before we made any drastic changes to our lifestyle. We accepted the invitation to come to Guyana.

Called or Crazy?

We were on our way! Were we crazy? After only two months of planning, getting a team together, gathering medical supplies, tickets, visas, and courage, we were finally on the plane headed to Guyana, South America. We would be among the first Americans to receive a visa since Jim Jones and his followers had made the world news almost 10 years ago. Scary thought! Yet this was an entirely different group with a radically different focus.

Our team consisted of Doug, an OB/GYN; Jo Mertz, a Pediatrician; Jeanine Larsen, RN; Terry Bennett, a pastor and me, an RN, among others.. We were followers of Jesus, not of a man, and we were heading towards this nation to be Jesus' ambassadors of love and healing, to give life and hope in practical ways.

This take-off felt different from others; we weren't going to Florida on vacation! We were leaving the familiarity and protection of our country and heading to a foreign land, one we had never been to before, and one we knew very little about. Yet we knew that we were in the hands of the One who was sending us.

Suddenly the lights vanished below and all I could see as I gazed out the window was the total blackness of the Atlantic Ocean by night.

"Doug, what are you thinking?" I asked pensively as I stared out into the dark abyss.

"I'm thinking I'm glad we're on the plane because I might get cold feet and change my mind. Jan, are we crazy or what? I sure hope we heard God, or this could be a very long month!"

I smiled slightly. *At least my man is honest*, I thought. I spoke a simple "Yeah" and we both closed our eyes and dreamed of the adventure awaiting us.

I awoke to daylight as we prepared for landing in Georgetown, the capital of Guyana. The view through my window quickly changed from the beautiful aquamarine of the ocean to a rich green jungle. Then I saw it! Just below us was an old concrete runway with grass and weeds poking up through the cracks. The airport terminal building looked old and dilapidated.

"Oh Doug," I began cautiously, "Are we going to land *here*? Look at this runway! It's not fit for landing. Surely this is a mistake, this isn't really the capital of the country?"

But there was no mistake; at least not about being at the right airport. All we could do was brace ourselves and wait, as we literally bumped and bounced across some awfully large cracks in the runway. We held onto our seats and tightened our seatbelts almost unconsciously. Then, just a couple of minutes later, we looked at each other and sighed with relief as we came to a halt. We were safe on the ground, and now the anticipation of all that lay ahead began to rise in my heart. *We're actually in Guyana. We made it. Lord, what kind of adventure are you taking us on with such a bumpy beginning?*

As we got out of the plane, the staring faces of army guards greeted us. They were all lined up in a row along the airport with machine guns in their arms. Why were they here? Why did they have guns? Talk about intimidating! We later learned that the country was paranoid of an attack. Our small team of seven fair-skinned Americans stood out among the disembarking planeload of dark-skinned Guyanese. *Should we be afraid?* I wondered. Somehow, this wasn't what I expected a mission trip would look like!

In the airport terminal building, people were pushing and shoving behind a mesh fence trying to get a glimpse of the disembarking passengers. It seemed everyone was yelling. Some held signs with names on them pushing them in the air to be seen by those arriving. The hot, humid, oppressive air felt like you just stepped into a sauna. The smell of body odor wafted our way – ugh!

Fortunately the Guyanese spoke English, a relief to have the familiarity of my own language, as this definitely was not an airport in Florida! We went through the customs and immigration with not only our personal suitcases but with 30 some boxes of medial supplies. This added to the tension, trying to juggle all the extra boxes.

Once on the other side of the mesh barrier we saw a young man holding up a sign with "Kinne" on it. It was a relief to see the promised government escort was waiting for us. Robin McLean was a tall, lean, good-looking, young man in his early twenties He was sent by the government to be our driver while we were in the country. It seems knowing someone who knows the president of the country has it advantages. Whew! He would know where to take us to get settled.

We loaded our luggage into a truck and settled into a van for our journey into Georgetown. We had scarcely started to travel when we both began to notice strange things.

"Did you see that cow in the road? We almost hit it!" I said as I clutched Doug's arm.

"I've never seen cows out roaming the streets. Look! Are those goats?" Doug exclaimed, hardly paying attention to me. Our curiosity heightened with each new and unfamiliar sight.

Houses were raised four or five feet off the ground, built up on stilts, for ventilation. Laundry was hanging to dry on a line strung up between the stilts. Three or four faded and tattered Hindu prayer flags perched next to many houses. Animals roamed freely everywhere.

The noise was intense. Roosters crowed, dogs barked, sheep baaed, and cows mooed. Little hawker stands with articles of clothing or fruits and vegetables on them lined the road into Georgetown. People were selling whatever they could to make a living. The smells of rotten fruit added to the culture shock we were all experiencing. The sides of the streets were lined with women and children in colorful clothing walking to town.

It must have been at least 90 degrees, quite a contrast from what we just left – frigid Northern Michigan in February. We dodged cows, people, and other varieties of animals for the next 40 minutes until we arrived in the city.

"This must be what they call sensory overload," I yelled to Doug over all the noise.

"Now I know for sure we are crazy," Doug hollered. However, I noticed a twinkle in his eyes and a smile on his face just the same.

Even the Birds of the Air have Nests

Judge Patterson still had a large house in Guyana that he offered our team to live in. I had visions of living in a mansion. We had been driving around the city for an hour trying to find the man who held the key to the mansion, but to no avail. "Guys, we can't find the caretaker who has the key to Judge Patterson's house," announced Doug to our very tired group. "But I have an idea." He dug for a piece of paper in his briefcase, and then went with Robin to make a phone call. They returned shortly.

"I found the name of Clarence Charles, a doctor who was listed in the Christian Medical Journal. I called him. He has offered to have us stay in his house. It's not the wonder house we were promised, but it's a roof over our heads." No one objected. By now, we didn't care about the large mansion we were promised. The consensus of the team was,

"Just get us a bed."

This turn of events turned out to be a real blessing. If we had lived in the mansion, we would have been far removed from the people. As we later learned, the perception was that we had dug in with the working class and were willing to live their lifestyle. This spoke volumes. We were available for folks to stop by our house where we shared the gospel with them. Isn't God good? He knew what was culturally appropriate and helped us, even down to our living quarters on our first day here.

We were anxious to settle into what would be our home for the next month. Dr. Clarence Charles lived in a modest white stucco house in the center of town. Spacious but sparsely furnished, barred windows looked cautiously out to a tall security fence where a guard was posted just outside for protection. We were told theft is a major problem, and a guard was necessary to protect our belongings and the contents of the house. Inside the fence, numerous chickens roamed, and roosters crowed.

Dr. Clarence Charles had just returned to Guyana and had not yet moved his family to Guyana from Trinidad, so we had our pick of rooms to sleep in. We plopped our luggage in the rooms, and followed our hungry stomachs to the kitchen. It didn't take long to discover that we couldn't find a single dish! *Didn't he ever eat here?* I wondered. What we did find was "cleanliness challenged." A shaken Dr. Jo Mertz, one of our team members exclaimed, "We can't stay here. Just look at this place. It's dirty! Bugs are everywhere!

And there aren't any dishes!" I really like things neat and clean so I wasn't thrilled either!

Doug, along with Terry, the only experienced missionary on our team, both used their great sense of humor to defuse the stress. They joked and tried to turn it all into a great adventure.

"Jo, just pretend you're camping" Doug said, as he pulled off a paper towel to use as a placemat. That night we ate Rice-a-Roni on paper plates on paper towels brought from home. The sight of our American medical team scooping up rice with our hands and licking it off with our mouths made us all laugh. I can't remember Rice-a-Roni ever tasting so good.

Ruined for the Ordinary

The next day we started work at the University hospital. The trip in from the airport was shocking, but it was nothing compared to seeing the hospital. This was supposed to be the best in the country! There were several large white buildings with the paint peeling, and windows with no screens. The huge wards held up to 30 beds, all lined up in rows. We soon noticed that most beds had two people in them – a head and two feet were visible from each end of the bed! I couldn't help but think that in our country, we complain if we don't have a private room. Here they even shared a bed!

Five medical students had been assigned to Doug to

mentor for his time there. They followed him throughout the wards as he made rounds on the patients. In surgery, he taught them new techniques. His love for teaching helped him to endure the otherwise taxing conditions. Flies, roaches, and rats wandered in the open wards. Sterilization was a joke. The interesting thing was the dirt didn't seem to matter to Doug. I noticed when he made rounds; he almost looked like he was having fun!

Later that evening while we were alone in our room, I asked Doug how he coped with the conditions he found in the hospital. With a great amount of passion in his voice he related, "This is what I went to medical school for, just to help people. It's great. I don't have to practice defensive medicine here. No lawyer is looking over my charts. I'm just helping people."

And that he did. Doug loved the patients, and he loved those students. He poured himself into them. They, in return, also loved him. He was ruined for the ordinary. I could sense a change coming over my husband. He was in his element, and he loved it. Sparks of joy were gradually building to a bright flame. I think this was my first indication that our lives would soon be changing.

Teamwork – Running Together

While Doug was busy with his work, I too was discovering how God might use me. Jeanine, the other nurse on the team and I were asked to teach nursing students. We found them eager to learn. I was an ICU nurse and had been told I would be given a chance to work in the ICU unit also. I was anxious to experience life as a nurse at this hospital. This was looking like it might be interesting after all. However, that was soon to change.

"Jan, come quickly to the ER," yelled Jilian, the head ICU nurse. On my first day in the ICU, an eighteen-year-old boy had just been brought into the ER. He was bleeding profusely from a stab wound to the abdomen.

"We must get his bandages clean before we can take him to the OR," Julian explained. I couldn't believe what I was seeing. Rather than taking him to the OR immediately, they kept trying to put new clean dressings on him. It was hard not to compare how we would have handled such a situation back home. Finally, I could stand it no longer.

"Could I start an IV? He needs his fluids replaced." I asked in the calmest voice I could muster, inwardly feeling frantic.

They let me start several IV's on him, but continued the futile effort to keep the bandages clean, postponing the much-needed entry into the operating room.

"I hope he knows Jesus," the respiratory therapist with me said, "cause it looks like he will meet Him soon if this keeps up!"

Finally, recognizing that their efforts were going nowhere, they wheeled him to the OR. Again, I was shocked at what I saw and heard. The workers fought over who would get to keep the gurney the patient was lying on. Would it go into the O.R. or would they move the patient to another gurney so the ER people could keep the gurney?

We later heard that the patient had died in the OR. My heart sank. *What a waste, an unnecessary loss of life*, I thought.   I was more upset then I thought and I asked Jeanine to pray with me that night. This likely wouldn't have happened in the US; the patient would most likely have lived because he would have been taken to the OR immediately and had surgery on the organ that was bleeding.

Yet, here I was in a strange and unfamiliar land. I needed to let go of my expectations, and fit into their culture and way of doing things.   Jeanine and I prayed a long time that night as I pondered, *do I really want to be a medical missionary after all…?*

If Necessary, Use Words

During the day, our medical team would work at the hospital or teach. We had not yet learned how to incorporate medicine and the gospel into our daily routine at work. Terry, our missionary and pastor, would make contacts with local pastors and arrange to speak at various meetings and churches. On Wednesday evenings and Sundays, we would go with him to his speaking engagements. (Christians do have a presence in Guyana along with Hindus and Muslims. Robin our driver professed to be Muslim, although we never saw him pray or attend a service while in Guyana.)

On church days, Robin would drive us to the church where Terry was scheduled to speak. At first, he would sit out in the car and listen to his music. After a few meetings, he came into the church and sat in the back. As time went on, we noticed he was moving further and further toward the front.

One night, a week from our departure date, Terry closed the evening service as he did every night, "I want to invite anyone to come forward who wants to invite Jesus to come into their heart – to ask Him to be their personal Savior." Robin nearly bolted out of his seat and flew up to the altar. He knelt, tears streaming down his face, while Terry prayed for him to accept Jesus into his heart. He later told us that he saw in us something that he wanted. Although we would talk with him about our faith, I believe he saw it lived out among us and this spoke louder than words. St. Francis of Assisi said, "At all times share your faith, if necessary use words."

Discovering God's Passion

Not only were we constantly experiencing new situations in our work, profound changes were happening to our lives and hearts on this trip. One day after long hours of working at the hospital, it was time for our nightly trip to the outdoor market. Since there was no refrigeration, we needed to buy food for dinner every evening. Back home, Doug generally hated shopping but here it was a great adventure.

It was like hunting, which he loved to do. I, on the other hand, just wanted to get what we needed and get out of there as quickly as possible. I didn't care for this kind of grocery shopping!

The sights and smells of the market were unlike anything we had ever experienced before. Dead chickens were hanging by their necks with swarms of flies on them. Mounds of colorful vegetables lined up in rows next to fish that smelled weeks old. People everywhere crowded together, shoving and pushing. The smell from all their bodies confirmed we were in a warm climate. We were white specks in a sea of black and brown faces and felt as out of place as we looked!

As we walked along, Doug suddenly stopped. I noticed in the midst of the commotion and crowds, he saw her, a girl about seven years old, a gypsy, likely one of the many street kids who hung out at the market hoping for a handout. Her dress used to be white but was now grimy and dirty, torn near the lace collar. The same dirt on her dress was also on her exposed arms and legs. She wore no shoes; her hair was curly and matted. Many had brushed her aside as a nuisance as she begged and disrupted their shopping.

She came up to him and tugged on his pant leg. I watched this exchange with fascination. They made eye contact.

"Mister, got some money? I need to eat." Big round brown eyes looking up at his tall frame pleaded even stronger than her tiny voice seemed to say, *"Won't you help me? Won't you give me something to eat?"*

Tears welled up in Doug's eyes. I don't remember what Doug did or said, but I do believe it was at that moment he discovered his passion…the lost, the outcasts, the ones nobody notices, the street children, the orphans. This passion drove him. He carried that passion in his heart for over 10 years until eventually he co-authored a class at our university called, Introduction to Children's Social Services. This class teaches others how to minister the love of Jesus to the disenfranchised children in the world. Doug had seen God's heart in the eyes of that child, and his life would never be the same. That day he not only discovered his passion, he became a missionary.

Watching that exchange, I too, wondered if this might be worth it! Something deep and profound seemed to be happening in my heart in spite of the conditions we were living in. I was beginning to feel this might be the "something more" we were searching for. Even little seemingly, unimportant happenings in our daily lives seem to confirm this.

Cribbage and Cockroaches

Back at our home base after evening dinner, Clarence, our host, recommended we not go out on the streets for safety. With nowhere to go and no TV to watch, we spent our evenings with each other. Our hearts bonded. Doug and Terry taught us how to laugh at difficult situations. They taught us to have fun. The littlest thing became a game.

"Eek!!" Jeanine, the other nurse on our team, shrieked as she pulled up her feet from the floor while sitting in a chair. We heard what sounded like a small herd of horses running across our hard wood floor. Another one! It was an enormous cockroach, the size of a playing card, scrambling across the floor. Jeanine screamed loudly, and inwardly I groaned.

"Don't worry about a thing" said Terry, our seasoned missionary. He pulled off his shoe and whacked the roach. "Whew!" we all groaned. Before long, another one approached. It had barely come into view when Jeanine threw a shoe and scored a perfect hit. In that instant, we invented our "Guyana Game," throwing shoes to see who could kill the most cockroaches! Our new "game" kept us entertained for many an evening.

Another favorite activity was the nightly cribbage games after dinner. The "South American Cribbage Championship" was born. The competition all started when our daughter, Tamara, joined us half way through our stay. She brought along a can of Pringle potato chips. Divided evenly, this came out to about eight chips per person. It was too much for Doug — his weakness was potato chips, and having gone weeks without one, he thought of a way to get more than his allotted portion.

"Jeanine, I'll challenge you to a cribbage game for your portion of the Pringles. Best two out of three."

"You're on," Jeanine responded confidently. "Cut to see who deals first."

"You should see my hand; boy, are those chips going to taste great!" Doug teased. "You're not going to get a good hand," he added a few moments later.

She was sure he was peeking at her cards. He didn't. He just knew how to "get her goat."

In the end, his words got into her head and badgered her, and he won. But, no matter – Jeanine later won the South American Cribbage Championship. Doug had won the potato chips though, and he never let her forget it!

The evenings at home in Guyana were like the evenings I remembered as a child; where families played games together and interacted with each other, without a TV set. We had fun without it costing any money either.

We were experiencing simplicity of life, and longed for it to continue. Back home it seemed we had lost that simplicity. But here, life didn't seem complicated. True, we had cockroaches, but we had something money couldn't buy – peace. I think we all silently pondered, *why can't it always be like this? Why can't it be like this at home?* At those moments, I truly didn't miss my home and its wonderful comforts.

Who Are The Poor Ones?

We were supposed to be the "rich Americans" working

in a poor country yet it was glaringly clear; we were the ones who were poor! The month passed quickly. It was now time to leave. Robin our driver, a Muslim, had asked Jesus into his heart, and became a Christian. We had grown to love these people. We had made a difference; we saw many changes for the better in a short amount of time. There was only one patient to a bed now. Many people came to know Christ as their Savior though our efforts in the churches and at the hospital. Even our house had become home, and the noisy roosters in the yard were friends rather than an irritation.

Even Jo, the one who thought the house was too dirty and full of bugs, got a new perspective. Towards the end of her time there, a big cockroach landed on her plate. Without missing a beat, Terry reached over and cut it in half.

"It was too big for one bite anyway," he told her. She laughed! Was this the same person who came with us? It seemed we all had changed.

Jilian, the nurse I worked with in the ICU, stopped by the house to say goodbye. "I can't believe you're leaving," she said. "It seems like you are one of us." I hugged her brown body and thought, *what a compliment. I don't look anything like her, yet she thinks I am one of her people.* I think that hug cemented it. I became a missionary.

As Robin was taking us to the airport for our flight home, a praise tape was playing in the van with the song, "Give Thanks With a Grateful Heart." The words rang into the stillness of the night. "…let the poor say I am rich, because of what the Lord has done for us, give thanks." Our eyes glistened with the stark realization; we were the ones who were poor. The cares and problems that once held us in their grip seemed trivial. We were not the same people that had flown into the country one month ago on that bumpy runway. We had changed. There would be no turning back!

Whoever said, "Go on a short term missions trip, it will change your life," was a wise person indeed!

Chapter 3

EARLY LIFE PATH:
Birth, School, Marriage and Family

"... He will direct your paths" (Proverbs 3:6).

Many times as we look back over our lives, we can see the hand of God, even if at the time we weren't aware of His presence. I have heard many people say, "I was raised to attend church, but have outgrown that now." Some say there are many ways to God, while others just don't find Him relevant in their lives. Sadly, in our affluent western society, many don't see a need for God.

St. Francis of Assisi said, "Our hearts are restless until we find rest in Him." If we are honest with ourselves, we all need to fill the God shaped-vacuum that is in us. Until we do, we may never be walking in the highest calling God has for us. As Mordecai told Queen Esther, "Who knows, maybe you were born for such a time as this?" (Esther 4:14).

A Son is Born

"It's a boy!" shouted Doug's father, Rex, on the day he was born, a snowy day in November in 1941. Finally, after waiting eight years and suffering several miscarriages since the birth of his daughter Joan, he had another child, a son. He was a big boy, weighing over nine pounds. It was after midnight following Halloween, a good day to have a son. It was All Saints Day on the church calendar, a day to honor those who have persevered for the cause of Christ. His parents named him Douglas George Kinne, George being his grandfather's name. What would this son become – the one who was born on such a special day?

Childhood

Doug's mother, Gladys, would take him to Sunday School every week at the Methodist church on the corner. He was a normal little boy – no saint, yet he won perfect attendance buttons for never missing a Sunday. His father loved baseball and wanted his son to love it too. They would go to all the local games and for a special treat, to see the Detroit Tigers. Doug would rather have had perfect attendance at the ballpark. He loved sports.

Doug's family ran the movie theater in their small town

of South Lyon, Michigan. From the late 1940s through the 1950s, he saw most of the Hollywood releases. He liked them all, but he especially liked westerns. His favorite actor was John Wayne. He thought, *"Here was a man who shoots first, asks questions later, and always got the girl."* John Wayne became Doug's idol and symbol of masculinity.

One day when he was eight years old, he was playing with a gang of boys. One of the boys punched Doug in the eye. (Knowing Doug, it may not have been without provocation.) Wham! A fist slammed into his eye. He started to cry. The neighbor boy taunted, "Look at the crybaby! Crying is for babies. Look at the baby."

Doug was humiliated and devastated. Though still a boy, he told himself, *"I'm a man and men don't cry, John Wayne would never cry."* From that point on, Doug vowed that he would never cry again. This innocent vow would shape his life for years to come.

He started out big at nine pounds, and by high school, he was 6 feet 4 inches and weighed 180 pounds. His size helped him excel in sports. He won letters in every sport he played, including football, basketball, and baseball. His sense of humor endeared him to others. He was in the school play. Still attending church, he was elected president of the Methodist Youth Fellowship. Loved by family, popular, smart, sought after by girls, life couldn't have been happier for Doug. However, his secure, happy life was about to change.

Instant Adulthood

"Doug, wake up!" His mother yelled as she stood over him shaking him out of a deep sleep. He awoke from a pleasant dream to suffer a real life nightmare. "It's your Dad. The ambulance is coming."

"Ma, what's wrong with Dad?" he whined, half awake as the ambulance pulled into the driveway.

"It's his heart. He's hurt'n real bad. Gotta run. Get ready for school. I'll let you know …." Her voice trailed off as she walked out the door.

It was February 1959, his senior year in high school. This day would forever change the course of his life. His dad had suffered a heart attack. Six days later, he was dead.

Things were never the same after that. His dad was his hero, his sports buddy, and his biggest fan at all his games. How could he go on without him? *Dad wouldn't be there to see him graduate. Who would run the theater? How would they make it with dad gone?* The enormity of it all sank into his soul. The happy, secure son became the man of the house, though not by choice.

Doug suddenly grew up with instant adult responsibilities. How could he comfort his mother while he felt a crushing ache in his inmost being? He had prayed so hard for God to make his dad well. Why would a loving God let his father die? Where was God now? Doug began to doubt God's existence.

A Change in Direction

Doug had mailed a letter to a Michigan congressman requesting recommendation for enrollment in West Point Academy.   He thought that admission there would be an easy and prestigious way for free tuition to college.   This dream would now have to be shelved.   How could he leave his mom and go to college in another state, miles away from home?

His sister lived in a nearby town, was married, and had a family.   She was expecting a baby.   She had enough on her plate.   When he received the letter saying that he was named an alternate, rather than receiving the appointment, it hardly mattered.   He had already determined he would need to be close enough to help his mother around the large old Victorian house, which now seemed even larger since dad wasn't there.   He decided to apply to the University of Michigan, a twenty-minute drive away.

A few weeks later, he waved an envelope from the University of Michigan in front of his mother.   "Yes! I'm accepted," he hollered.   His mother beamed with pride, and Doug just couldn't contain his joy.   This gave him some of the independence he yearned for. It was only a short drive home to help his mother when she needed it. Things were looking up for this new stage in his life, everything except for one little thing – college tuition.   With Dad gone, the family income wasn't what it used to be. *How would he pay college tuition?*   He was soon to see how God would provide.

God's Invisible Hand

The answer came initially through a part-time job, working with Dr. Bean, a biochemist in a research lab at the University. Doug had saved the money he earned working for his dad in the theater. Together with this job in the lab and his savings, he had gotten through almost three years of college, but finances were running out.

In the long hours of the night, hunched over microscopes and Petri dishes, his interest in medicine emerged. His thoughts of life as a professional athlete/officer at West Point faded as he embraced the idea of becoming a physician. That meant an additional four more years in medical school. *How could he afford that?* He still had a year of college left to complete. After that, his money would run out. Again, God demonstrated His faithfulness to a wounded young man, who hadn't given Him a thought in over three years.

In the spring of Doug's junior year of college, Doug was working in the lab when Dr. Bean, entered and interrupted his thoughts.

"Doug, remember you talked to me about going to medical school? Were you serious?"

"Sure was, but I don't see how I can afford it. Tuition is expensive you know.

I only have enough money left for one more year of school."

"What would you say if I told you I'll recommend you

to the accelerated program here at the University? If they accept you, you can enter medical school after this year and skip your last year of college. Sometimes in special cases they do that. What do you think? Do you want to go to medical school this fall?"

Doug just stared at him as the reality of his words sunk in. "Can you really do that?" He was barely able to get the words out. The financial implications of this announcement were enormous. *Skip a year of tuition? Once he was in medical school, he would then be eligible for medical school scholarships. This might just work!*

"Okay, let's go for it," said Doug excitedly.

"I'll see what I can do; let's give it a try. We just might get you in." Dr. Bean smiled as he walked out the door.

"Thanks!" Doug managed to say, as Dr. Bean left. He was still in a daze. *Is this really happening?* he thought. Time would tell.

Till Death Do Us Part

My two roommates and I had just moved to Ann Arbor the week before. We had been out of nursing school for one year, had all broken up with boyfriends, and had moved to this college town to start a new life. A friend had told me, "All these medical students in Ann Arbor are just waiting to meet good looking nurses." Since we were nurses, this sounded good to us! Here we were!

"I'm stuck in the snow. Could you guys give me a hand?" I asked at the door of the end apartment, the one closest to the parking lot. I was on my way to Wednesday night Lenten service and couldn't get out of the parking lot. I needed a push!

Doug, a first year medical student, lived in this apartment building with two others just two doors down from us. We had noticed them when we moved in, as we struggled, carrying boxes past their window as they sat at the table studying. *What jerks*, I thought, *they could at least help us!*

I wasn't sure they would help me now. They still looked very busy studying. Maybe I looked as helpless as I felt. To my surprise Doug replied, "We'll get our coats and be right out. Sounds like you could use a push."

I sighed. *Maybe they weren't jerks after all.*

Then Doug added, "We'll give you a push if you and your roommates will come over for coffee when you get home."

"You're on," I said excitedly. Things were definitely looking up at our new location. I couldn't wait to tell my roommates about the invitation.

"Lois, Josie!" I yelled to my two roommates as I walked in the door. "You won't believe what happened to me. I got stuck in the driveway on my way to church. You know those guys in the end apartment? Well, I knocked on the door and asked them to give me a push. They said they would give me one, if when I got home I'd get you two and come for coffee. They want us to come over in a few minutes. Well? Wanna go?"

"Josie's at the neighbor's using the phone since ours isn't hooked up yet," said Lois. "I'll go though. That one guy's kinda cute!"

Just then, Josie returned. We told her about our invitation. She started to laugh.

"One of those guys just came to the neighbor's door while I was there, asking if he could borrow some coffee!"

Lois screeched, "This is too funny. Did he act embarrassed when he saw you?" We all laughed – all the way to the guys' apartment.

Doug's roommate, another medical student, answered the door.

"Hi, I'm George Schaub and the guy with the red face holding the coffee is Doug Kinne."

We all laughed, including Doug. I knew I liked him. He could laugh at himself!

Our First Date

"Jan's had an accident!" Lois, my roommate announced to Doug as he came to pick me up me for our first date a few weeks later. I walked out into the living room to greet him, sporting the black eye I had gotten on the ski hill the night before. Doug thought I looked hilarious. I was embarrassed; I looked so ugly! He didn't seem to mind. We laughed as we walked in the door at the party with his friends. I'm sure I was a very impressive looking date!

He called me again and again. We took long walks. He didn't have any money for dates, yet I thought this poor medical student was so special. Maybe he didn't have money, but he had character. We were falling in love. We began to discuss our dreams for the future. During one of those talks I said, "Doug, someday I would like to be a medical missionary."

"That's nice. I would too, but I don't think that will work. You see, I think I'm an atheist!" My heart sank. This nice guy, an atheist! Did I hear him right?

He went on, "I don't think I believe in God any more. I don't think a loving God would have let my dad die." He then told me his story about his dad and how his death had been for him. I appreciated his honesty. It was apparent that he had really been hurt.

My heart went out to him but I had to be honest about my convictions.

"I don't think I can marry anyone who isn't a Christian. I couldn't love someone so much, spend my life with him and know that we wouldn't spend eternity together."

This led to many hours of discussion. He wanted to

believe again. He acted as if he wanted me to say something to change his mind about God's existence and love for him. Now he was the one who was stuck! But, unlike me back in that snow, he was having a hard time getting out. He was stuck in past pain. I couldn't do anything to help him; this was something he would have to work out himself. I could only tell him that God still loved him.

He started going to church with me. God was touching the hurting boy inside. One day in late spring he told me, "I believe."

We were married that fall, his second year of medical school.

From Dad to Doc

Doug didn't need to worry about tuition now. He had a working wife, at least until our first son, Rex, was born. Having a child meant less time for me to work, and money got tight again.

We worked hard to get Doug through school. Doug worked at the hospital many late nights, sitting with unruly patients. This allowed him to get some studying done when they finally did sleep. Doug's mom stayed with our son Rex, while I worked part-time in the afternoons. We lived on $3,000 dollars a year and $1,500 hundred of that was tuition!

The day finally came when I dressed Rex (named after

Doug's father) in his finest. He was too young to understand what this day meant, yet he watched as his daddy walked down the isle to receive his M.D. degree. Doug had done it! He had graduated from medical school. God was watching. I wonder if his dad was too.

Our son Matthew was born at the end of Doug's year of Internship. He soon guessed that he was about to be drafted into the Vietnam War, so he signed up for the U.S. Air Force. He realized another dream when he was commissioned as a Captain, serving as a General Medical Officer. Upon completion of his duty, he entered a four-year residency in OB/GYN at the University of Michigan. God continued to be faithful to supply all our needs during those years. Tamara, our youngest, came along at the end of his residency. Our family and his schooling were finally completed -- 14 years after the ambulance came to get his dad.

Finally Arrived

Pe-tos-key, where is that? We couldn't even say it! However, this small town of 6,000 in Northern Michigan was to become our new home. It was a summer/winter resort area on Lake Michigan. In 1973, Doug joined the Burns Clinic, then a clinic of 50 specialists in various medical fields (unheard of for a town its size). We bought a beautiful 3,700 sq. ft. home just outside the city, on a hill overlooking Lake Michigan and two other inland lakes. It had five bedrooms and three baths. The kids each had their own room. Life was good. We had finally arrived. I didn't know it then, but something was still missing.

A New Life

We had taken the youth group from our church to Traverse City, a town a little over an hour's drive away. We were going to a David Wilkerson Crusade. David had written a book, *The Cross and the Switchblade*. We were told that he appealed to youth.

"Who wants to accept Jesus Christ as their personal Savior? Maybe you have already, but you want to be sure of your salvation. Come forward. Come make a declaration before the world that you accept Jesus Christ as your Savior," called David Wilkerson from the stage at the crusade, following his message.

To my amazement, Doug nearly flew out of his chair, took my hand and went forward. There David prayed for each person. As he prayed for Doug, the floodgates opened. All those bottled up tears he vowed he would never cry spilled out onto his cheeks, running down on his collar. He cried like a baby, and this time he didn't care who saw him! Never mind what John Wayne had said; God was doing a healing work.

When Doug finally got his composure after all those tears, he looked at me.

"Just wanted to make sure," he said. I hadn't known he wasn't sure. I do know he was never the same after that night. He had a new zeal for the Lord.

It would be quite a few years later before our first short term missions experience. The Lord continued to weave together the events in our lives, using each step, each phase as a preparation for the next.

God had taken him a very long way from that day his dad died. Longer still, from the day he was born. Yet, God still had paths He wanted to direct this special doctor on, the one born on All Saints Day.

Chapter 4

PREPARING FOR A NEW LIFE PATH:

Skill Development

*"He is no fool who gives what he cannot keep,
to gain what he cannot lose."*
Jim Elliott

It was January 1991, and once again I found myself
looking out the window of an airplane, wondering *where in
the world we were about to land.* This time the problem
wasn't the runway. It looked just fine. My fantasy of Hawaii
being one big beach quickly dissipated as I saw the beautiful
aquamarine blue ocean fading in favor of acres and acres of
black lava rock surrounding the airport. It looked more like

we were arriving on the moon than in Hawaii! Where were the beautiful beaches one usually associates with Hawaii? It's a good thing we didn't come to Hawaii for the beach! We were now becoming full-time missionaries.

At the airport we waited for our ride. Soon a van pulled up with a University of the Nations sign in the window. A fellow with a big smile opened the door and stepped out to greet us, "Hi, I'm Stew, one of the staff from Crossroads; I'm here to take you to Makapala." A handful of others emerged from the crowd of people at the airport to join us for the 60-mile trip to our destination, a former retreat center on the north end of the island that was now a training extension center run by the University of the Nations' main campus in Kona. The University of the Nations is one of many bases around the world run by "Youth with a Mission" (YWAM).

An hour or so later the van pulled into what would be our home for the next three months. A huge green lawn surrounded many cabins used to house staff and students; a large, stately banyan tree stood off to the left to the road, as if it was saying, "Come on in." On the perimeter various colors of yellow, red, pink, and peach flowers confirmed we were indeed in Hawaii; the lush foliage and abundant flowers were entirely different from the "moonscape" visible from the plane window. Now it seemed we were in Hawaii, a quiet and restful place where we were about to experience the beginning of a whole new way of life.

While this was not the campus we originally applied to, we knew we were just where God had placed us. It was five miles to the nearest town and two miles from the end of the road. God had a better plan for us by bringing us to this location instead of to the main campus. It didn't matter to us at that point where we were; we knew that God had clearly paved the way for us and had confirmed His leading. All the events and concerns we had dealt with to get here seemed remote. Nevertheless, as I look back on it, I am amazed at how God got us to this point.

Leaving Home

One of the things we had to consider early on was how to deal with all our possessions, and how to disengage from all our responsibilities, particularly our jobs. We had two houses, four boats, four cars, and two dogs! We were also concerned about college for the kids and aging parents. By then, we had been on a few short-term mission trips, but what would it take to go into mission work full time?

It wasn't that we wanted to hold on to everything; we had experienced a better way of living, free from all our "stuff" and yearned for that "uncluttered" life. We just didn't know what to do next. We prayed, and as we waited on the Lord, He seemed to be saying "Simplify your life!" Though we didn't know how, we figured that there must be a way if that's what the Lord was leading us to do. We learned the hard way. We made a plan, but, because we didn't consult God, it didn't work.

One day Doug went to work and made a proposal to

his partners.

"What would you say if I worked six months a year, and took six months off so I can do my mission work?" Doug asked. We thought that this was the perfect plan since it costs very little to live in a developing nation. It seemed to be workable for us and for the clinic.

Jack, the OB/GYN Department Head replied, "You know we really could use another person in the department. We are so busy, especially during summer when the tourists are all here. How would it work for you if we hired another full-time person and you worked the six months of summer when we are the busiest?"

"Perfect," Doug answered. The decision was made. We had a plan and all that had to be done was to find his replacement. The clinic advertised in all the medical periodicals, and even used agencies to help find a replacement for him. Nothing seemed to be working.

While the search went on, we continued to take short-term missions trips. We went back to Guyana and also to Trinidad and Tobago a year later. We became increasingly impatient. The "rat race" was closing in on us again. It had been two years since that decision was made with his partners.

Yet, as hard as they tried to find a replacement, none was forthcoming. Our plan of working six months in missions work and six months in Doug's regular job never came to fruition. In the late spring of 1990, as we prayed about the problem, we sensed that the Lord was saying that we had followed our own ideas, not His. We were soon to find out what that meant.

Is That Really You God?

Not long after we had prayed about our dilemma, the singing group Gentle Touch Ministries (GTM) came to our church. They called themselves "Musicianaries." They used their music as they ministered behind the Iron Curtain. My heart was stirred while they were singing. I remembered our own missionary experiences and was anxious to get back into that lifestyle. I can't explain it, but somehow after that service, I just knew that the end of the year was the time for us to make our move, and that we were not to keep waiting for Doug's replacement at the hospital.

That afternoon Doug and I were having a relaxing time together out in our boat. With one of those rare moments we had to be alone, I thought this was a good time to talk about what had happened that morning. I knew he couldn't walk out of the boat, so I asked.

"Doug, did you feel anything today at church?"

"Yeah, I did." Then, almost apologetically, he continued. "Now this is going to sound funny, but during the service I sensed that God was saying we needed to leave at the end of the year." My heart leapt. I couldn't believe what I was hearing.

"That's what I sensed too!" I quickly responded with

excitement.

To think that God was telling us both the same thing that morning left us both dumbfounded and in awe of God.

One might think that such an incident would have been enough to let us know it was God talking to us, but we still had to be sure. This was a big step we were about to take. It's not a light thing to quit a well-paying job as a physician, especially in a small town where there didn't seem to be an eminent replacement.

The following evening we invited the singing group GTM over for dinner to tell them what we had sensed from the Lord and to ask a few questions.

"How do you know for sure this is the will of God and not just my own desire?" Doug asked Jim one of members.

"Well," Jim began, "one way I describe the will of God is it's like a lingering persuasion that will not go away until you do something about it."

"Hmmm," said Doug pensively. "We certainly haven't been able to get rid of this thought about going into missions full-time. What else?"

"If you check your heart and see that you really want God's will above all else, God sees that and He then gives you the desire of your heart. He knows your heart is His. When He puts His desires in your heart, they are in line with His will," Jim said.

"That all makes sense so far," I piped in. "What about our kids, our parents, our stuff? If this is God leading us, how do we deal with all those issues?" Though we wanted to serve God full time, the idea was a little daunting. It meant no more income. Retiring early meant we couldn't access Doug's pension until he turned 55, and that was another six years away. What about health insurance? We would lose that if we left. How could we afford this transition? "This time of questioning brought up the point of asking, "Is that really you God speaking to us?"

"It'll work out," Jim assured us. "I don't have all the answers to your questions. But I know that if this desire is from God, He will work it all out." "This time of questioning brought us to the point of asking, "Is that really you God speaking to us?"

With many questions unanswered, we continued to move forward. We remembered a friend who owned a small business, sold it and went into missions, only to return to the business world when things got a little difficult. We wanted to make sure this was God's will for us. We didn't want to turn back! Doug met with the elders of our church. He told them that we both believed that the Lord was leading him to quit his job at the clinic at the end of the year in order to become full-time missionaries. He asked them to pray on our behalf.

Two weeks later, they came back to Doug and said that if we felt we had heard God, then we should go, and they promised to stand behind us in our decision.

When Doug shared this with me, I thought about a book I had read, *Take Another Look at Guidance*, by Bob Mumford. In it Bob states there are three things that must line up, sort of like buoys in a harbor, if something is God's will: The Word of God, the Holy Spirit, and circumstances. I had also heard that peace always comes with God's leading. We looked at how the Lord had led us.

We knew God said in His Word, "Go into the entire world and preach the gospel." Secondly, the Holy Spirit had clearly given both of us a hunger for ministering in a world beyond our city, i.e., He was speaking to our hearts by giving us a desire to do this new thing. With this last confirmation, both of us "knew" the time for us to make this change was the end of the year. All the "buoys" lined up. Doug and I processed this together. The decision was made. We were in agreement. He gave his resignation to the clinic, and. I submitted my resignation to the hospital, both to become effective Dec.31, 1990.

Pressured to Stay – Peers and Patients

While the financial issues were obvious hurdles to get over, they weren't the only ones. Doug's peers and patients put pressure on him to stay at the clinic. Some of the staff thought he must be crazy; others expressed doubt that he would really do it. Many of the women who had been patients of Doug's wondered what they would do without him. Most women just love their obstetrician. Almost daily

Doug heard the pleading, "Don't go. What am I going to do without you?" He was honored by the attention, but knew that "Someone" greater than his patients had given him a far more compelling plea, "Go!"

Dealing with Doubts

We had to battle personal doubts about our own fitness and profile as missionaries. We thought a missionary had to go to seminary for three years and do language acquisition. We had to overcome the perceptions and misconceptions of the missionary stereotype as seen in history books. It isn't necessarily so. We had to discover how missionaries live and operate in the late 20th Century.

Even our own family questioned this call on our lives. While supportive, our kids expressed concern. They worried about our safety. Although they were all living on their own and didn't really need us, I think they just wanted the comfort and security of having us in the house where they grew up. We understood their concerns and talked with them. However, we had to obey the call being issued to our hearts.

Breaking the Ties

Another issue that came up during the two years of our waiting had to do with Doug's mother. We noticed that she seemed to get sick every time we were about to leave the country. One of those times, Doug went to visit his mom in the hospital. He decided to talk with her about her response to our going out.

"Mom, why did you send me to Sunday School? Why did I earn all those perfect attendance buttons? Didn't you raise me to learn about and share my faith? Don't you want me to embrace the will of the Lord?"

Surprised and humbled, she answered, "Yes."

Doug continued. "Mom, would you pray with me? Would you release and commission me for full-time service to the Lord?" She agreed immediately, and after that prayer, she was never sick again when it was time for us to leave, although she did have chronic health issues.

As the end of the year drew near, we had no idea what we were going to do. For both of us this was a stretch. We were long-range planners. However, we felt unprepared to go into full time missions without a clear game plan. We were two zealous, skilled people with a desire to serve God, but with nowhere to go.

Where Now Lord?

Praying about our next step, I had seen a picture in my mind of where I thought we were supposed to go. Matt, our son had gone through a Discipleship Training School (DTS) with Youth with a Mission (YWAM), and had been given the book, "*Is That Really You, God?*" by YWAM's founder,

Loren Cunningham. The book was sitting on the kitchen table, and on the back cover, I saw a picture of Loren and his family by the water.

I said to myself, *"That's it. That's where we are supposed to be.* Where was that picture taken?" The book said Kona, Hawaii. I thought, "Great, I'd like to go to Hawaii but isn't YWAM for young people? What about middle-aged people like Doug and me?"

We called the Youth With A Mission training center in Kona, Hawaii and inquired about training programs for us. We were delighted to discover that they had a program for people over 35, called Crossroads Discipleship Training School (CDTS). The name certainly fit our situation – we were definitely at a crossroads in our lives. We learned that the program is designed for people just like us – people who sense God is calling or might be calling them to make a change in how they use their gifts in His kingdom. The five-month course in two parts (three months of classroom training and two months of a cross-cultural mission outreach with the whole class) is based on the motto of YWAM: "To know God and make Him known."

We would receive training in the Word of God then be taught how to share our faith cross-culturally, testing and putting into action the principles taught in the first phase, working alongside someone experienced in missions. This would give us the training we felt we lacked. This "over-35" group is taught how to use the life skills they already have in a new context, one that is generally in a less developed, less evangelized part of the world. A feature of this program we were also attracted to was that, if after completion of it we felt this wasn't the path for us, we weren't "stuck" in a commitment for two or more years. We would be free to move on and wouldn't have wasted years in training and language acquisition. This seemed like the perfect fit for our needs.

We received encouragement to take this program from Jim Manthei, a friend and one of the elders at our church. "Doug, I think it is a good idea to take the five-month training program. It would be a good bridge between the working world and the uncertain, no-income world of missions." We didn't have all our answers yet, but this seemed like wise counsel. God appeared to be leading us down this path.

We did the next thing we knew to do. We applied and were accepted into the Crossroads class in Kona, Hawaii, which was to begin in early January 1991.

God's Provision: One Step at a Time

A month before we were to leave, I resigned from my job as a RN in ICU and shortly thereafter received an unexpected phone call.

"Jan, this is Cheryl calling from Ypsilanti." Cheryl had been my best friend for years. "Sam and I have decided to move back up north this January. We'd like to be there for our kids to start school their second semester. Do you know of any place that we might rent until we can find our own place?"

I couldn't believe what I was hearing. With enthusiasm I instantly replied, "Yes I do – our place!" I began to tell her of our plans, and it wasn't long before she and Sam decided to rent our home. Things were falling into place in ways we couldn't have imagined. With the rental of our house, our larger expenses were mostly taken care of. We had decided that for now we would keep our house and "stuff" until we had a clear direction on where we would go next. There would be time later to make a decision once we knew our long-range plans.

Another concern we had along the way was what to do about health insurance. We were told about the Cobra Plan, a way to keep one's health insurance for 18 months after leaving a job. It meant we had to pay the premiums, but the Lord made a way for us to do that too. We decided to discontinue the life insurance plan. Bit by bit, we could see God was indeed taking care of all the details that had worried us. We were in awe of His hand and provision.

Be Flexible

Not long after we had been accepted to the Crossroads DTS, I received a phone call from Hawaii.

"Hello, this is Millie, calling from Kona. I just wanted to let you know that the class that you registered for is larger than we expected, so we've had to split the class. You will be going to our campus at Makapala, 60 miles north of the main campus at Kona; just thought you'd like to know."

"Doug, we're not going to Kona!" I lamented that evening as he came in the door.

"Jan, it's all right. God knows what He's doing," he said.

We were disappointed but willing to accept the decision. I don't think we had a choice. Things weren't turning out as I had thought! *What happened to the picture I saw in my mind, the one on the book cover?* I thought. Before we had begun this new venture, God was beginning our training. He was teaching us about flexibility, a major aspect of the missionary life.

Obstacles

I was told that once you make a decision to serve God, Satan gets angry, and not to be surprised when problems surface, sometimes several at a time, just as you are preparing to launch into something new. This proved to be the case with us.

It was early December. Doug had decided that he should have a long overdue hernia repair before we left. It was scheduled for 7:30 a.m. Tuesday morning.

Though he had finished college, Matt was home for a season, temporarily living with us. He had taken the dogs to the vet that morning to be neutered. While he was out doing that, I drove to the hospital to pick up Doug after he had spent the night caring for patients, and had gone straight from work to the operating table for his surgery, without first coming home. After his outpatient surgery, I brought him home in our car, leaving his truck at the hospital.

His mother, who was recovering from a stroke, had come to spend time with him while he recovered from his hernia repair. We were all settled back at the house when I asked his mother to help out.

"Mom," I said to her, "can you get Doug anything he might need? Henry, Doug's friend, had come to take me to the hospital to pick up Doug's truck. Also, would you call Matt at school and ask him to pick up the dogs at the vet on his way home? Thanks." I yelled, as I walked out the door.

In the hospital parking lot, I found Doug's truck. On the way home, I decided that I would stop at the print shop. As I stepped out of the truck, wham! My feet flew out from under me as I turned my ankle and fell to the ground. There was a little patch of ice by the curb and I found it! I winced as my left foot pounded with pain. *Oh God what do I do?*

I was by myself, and my husband was in bed recuperating. Even though I was in extreme pain, I decided to crawl up into the truck. The truck had an automatic transmission. Since it was the left foot that was injured, I managed to drive back to the hospital. Outside the emergency room door, I pushed on the horn until one of the male nurses came outside.

He recognized me. "Jan, what's wrong?" he exclaimed?

"I think I broke my foot. I can't walk. Help me!" He brought out a wheelchair, took me inside and had someone else park the truck.

The x-rays revealed that I had broken a small bone in my foot. I had also wrenched my knee pretty badly. The doctor decided to send me home and postpone casting it until after the swelling went down. I called my pastor to come and get me. I couldn't drive after taking a pill for the pain.

Back at home, Doug's mom met me at the door. I explained what happened, and then hobbled straight to the bedroom.

"Doug, move over. I broke a bone in my foot. I need to lie down." He managed a weak groan for answer. With that, I snuggled in next to him and fell asleep.

I awoke to Matt's voice. "Mom, Dad, move over. I've got some more cripples to join you." He picked up the two dogs and put them on our bed with us. They were too sore to jump up by themselves. The four of us lay there, resting, healing, and groaning together!

The Journey Begins

On January 1, 1991, we boarded the plane at our local

airport. We were Hawaii bound, but not for a vacation! Our kids, friends, and church family were all present to send us off with their blessings.

Changing planes in Detroit, we were a funny sight. I had just gotten my cast off. Doug had to push me in a wheelchair between gates. When we got to our gate, I got out of the wheelchair, picked up our carryon bag, and hobbled onto the plane while Doug followed along behind me. He could push me in a wheelchair, but he wasn't allowed to lift more than 15 pounds following his surgery. To the unwary passerby, it probably looked like he was making his crippled wife carry the luggage! We laughed. It didn't matter; what was important was that we had done it – we had left our jobs and followed our hearts, being led by God. We were on our way to Hawaii and a new life. A new life indeed and we were almost 50!

The Perfect Place – Makapala

Our new home was indeed remote and not at all like the picture. But we settled into the routine of the school and were glad to be there.

Several weeks after starting our class, Doug and I packed our lunch and walked across the street to a field next to a cliff overlooking the ocean. We put our blanket down. There was little else to do here on a Sunday. No place to go. This was a peaceful beautiful spot. Doug was reading the Bible to me when he suddenly remarked, "God...I'm so happy."

I looked over at him quizzically, "Why is that?"

"I haven't slept every night, all night, this many days in a row, in over 25 years. This is great!" A huge smile lit up his face.

I hadn't thought about it. Babies don't respect your sleep schedule when they're ready to be born. At first, it had been hard being so isolated, but God knew what we needed. He had taken us out of the "Rat Race" and slowed us down. We soon realized how close to burnout we had been. We soaked up all the wonderful teaching. Furthermore, after years of seeing our Christian friends only once or twice a week, we were able to fellowship with like-minded Christians daily. We formed some deep and lasting friendships.

Since Doug and I both were very driven people, Makapala proved to be the very place we needed to be – remote, with only one TV in the dining room that was turned on half an hour each day for the news. We were told most schools aren't in such a remote area. It seemed that God had placed us just where we needed to be. Now we could see the wisdom of God in sending us here rather than to the main campus in Kona.

The "lecture phase" was like sitting at the feet of Jesus. We couldn't have set aside that kind of time while working in our jobs. It was wonderful to have this time set apart to listen to Jesus, to allow Him to do a deep work in our hearts. As I look back on it, I wouldn't have wanted to go into missions without this time in the lecture phase. It settled us down and gave us some skills that I still use today. Our future ministry would have been poorer had we not taken the time to renew our minds.

One profound teaching I remember by Joe Ferrante, a pastor from California, was on "The Extravagant Love of the Father," speaking of God's character, emphasizing His heart toward us as a loving Father.

"If you are truly seeking to do the will of God and think He told you to do something and miss it, He doesn't hit you on the side of the head, say 'you dummy,' and leave you forever because you blew it! He loves you, is patient with you, and gently draws you back to Himself," said Joe, with all the love and compassion of God reflected in both his voice and eyes.

It was good to have this truth reinforced, especially as we were truly seeking the will of God and "stepped out" into something new, even though many friends and colleagues seemed to think that we had missed it. If we had made a wrong decision, God still loved us and had a plan for our lives, and would gently lead us.

Lessons Applied

Following the "lecture phase" it was time for "outreach" – a two to three month application time. As a group, we were to go on a mission's trip to apply the lessons learned, a time of demonstrating the love of Christ, and telling others what He had done in our lives. We would go to a country in Asia (name withheld for security reasons), Hong Kong, and Okinawa. I wondered, *would we be able to share our faith any better than before?* I would soon find out.

A New Kind of Test

We were in a country where the major religions are Islam, Christianity, and Hinduism. (Country withheld for security reasons.)

Our team was small – just six of us. Tom and Willa Brook were about 10 years older than we were, and Gene and Terry Schaff were 10 years younger. We all had previous mission experience and were hand picked for this particular mission. Since Doug and I had led outreaches before, we were put in charge as student leaders.

"Find the Christians, start a church." That was the charge given us by our outreach leaders as they dropped us off in a fishing village. They also told us, "Find a place to live. You have two weeks. Then we will be back for you!"

We lived in a Guesthouse, centrally located in the middle of town. The owner was Hindu. There were Hindu gods in all the main rooms. We were awakened early every morning by the local *muezzin* (one who calls Muslims to prayer) as he shouted over the loudspeakers in the wee hours of the morning, and again at sundown (and other times in between!). It was Ramadan, the highest Muslim religious holiday. We were definitely in unfamiliar territory.

We had been told that two Christians lived in this village. They would be the nucleus for our church. How would we find them? In this culture, it wasn't appropriate or advisable to ask if someone was a Christian. In fact, it could put their life in danger – and ours too! It was against the law to proselytize. We could end up in prison or worse! We appeared to be the only westerners in the village. Would they suspect the reason we came? This assignment definitely would require prayer and a lot of wisdom from God.

Doug, Tom and Gene developed a ministry playing ping-pong at a drug rehabilitation center. The man in charge of the inmates started asking questions about God. Telling people about the Lord and playing ping-pong frequently was about as much fun as Doug could have asked for. Before we left the country, many from the center asked Christ into their hearts.

Willa, Terry, and I went to the beach. We were just sure we would meet people there who needed to be saved! Mostly though, we walked around the town praying – praying for the people to know Christ, praying for an opportunity to tell them about Him. Open evangelism was not allowed, so we prayed and waited to see what opportunities would open up to us.

We had worship every morning before going out for the day. One day we noticed our Hindu friend's 15-year-old daughter watching us intently.

"Come join us," Doug said.

'No, no, it just sounds so beautiful. Why do you always look so happy?" she inquired.

"Because we have Jesus living in our heart," Doug replied.

"How do I get this Jesus in my heart?" she asked.

We didn't know what to do. She was the daughter of the owner of this house. How would he ever believe we didn't proselytize her? In this nation, proselytizing was a crime. But, she had asked and we had to tell her.

She accepted Jesus that day, but didn't tell her parents until years later. (For ten years, we received letters from her each Christmas reaffirming her growing faith.)

One day towards the end of the two weeks, Tom had gotten flu-like symptoms, so he stayed in for the afternoon. He agreed to pray. He was a great intercessor.

"It's Thursday. We leave on Sunday. Pray we find the Christians today." I told him, as the rest of us prepared to go out. "Time is running out." He stayed to pray while we walked around town. By evening, he was feeling better, so he decided to take a walk with Willa on the beach. As they walked, a woman and her son came up to them. They noticed the woman was wearing a cross.

"Are you a Christian?" asked Willa. "I noticed the

cross you are wearing."

Her name was Martha* and her 10-year-old son was named John the Baptist! They had been praying God would send someone to help them start a church. Tom suggested that she get some interested people together and our team would come to speak to them.

The next night we arrived at Martha's house to find 30 people, all eager to hear about the Lord. From that group a church was formed. That church is still going today. Perhaps this is not the typical way to start a church, but we did what we could and left the results to God.

And to think we ever questioned leaving the security of work, home, stuff, and all that was familiar! We were making a difference in people's lives – for eternity, not just by providing medical care.

Jim Elliot, the young missionary pilot who was murdered by the Auca Indians of South America, was right:

"He is no fool who gives what he cannot keep,
to gain what he cannot lose."

Chapter 5

UNCHARTED PATH:

Opening a Closed Country

"The gates of hell will not prevail against it"
(Matthew 16:18).

The Call

Most people would jump at the chance to serve God in Hawaii. Wasn't missions supposed to be pith helmets and hardships, not the Hawaiian tradition of leis and leisure?

Once, years ago, one of the cartoon characters from *Peanuts* said amid falling snowflakes, "When I grow up I want to be a missionary to Hawaii." I thought, *how nice of God to call us back to Paradise.* Little did we know that our stay in Hawaii was a mere stepping-stone from almost Heaven to almost Hell!

The year following our training, we returned to the University of the Nations (U of N) in Kona, Hawaii. We came back to teach and direct student medical training for a 12-week intensive "school" called "Applied Primary Health Care." The U of N operates on a modular system where students take only one intensive class at a time.

In this advanced level course, students are trained to be clinicians. When they finish the course, they are able to treat 80% of the most common medical problems in the world. They learn how to dress wounds, deliver babies, set broken limbs, extract teeth, and even suture.

As the students and staff of the school were praying about where to go on outreach, the Lord reminded someone of the scripture from Acts 16:9 "Come over to Macedonia and help us." That same day an email arrived from Albania asking us to consider bringing a team there. We looked at the map in the back of the Bible and to us; it looked like Albania used to be a part of Macedonia! Excited at this clear call, we were also concerned. This formerly Communist country had been closed for over 50 years. Was this where we were to take the gospel? However, God had clearly given us the call.

Darkness to Light

The Berlin Wall was finally opened by East Germany on November 9, 1989 and torn down by the end of 1990 as Communism collapsed and the Cold War ended. In November 1991 at the death of Communist dictator Enver Hoxha, Albania opened up to the outside world. For the previous 50 years, it had been a Communist country, and Hoxha had taken great pride in declaring Albania an atheistic country. He announced to the world that he had successfully expunged all religions from his country.

Greek Orthodox and Islam were the two main religions practiced up until then. Under Communism, all the churches and mosques closed. Now, they served as museums or Communist headquarters for the area.

We would be taking our health care school into Albania for their three-month practicum where we would run medical clinics in the rural areas. Patients would hear about Jesus and be offered a New Testament Bible in their own language. That was the plan.

Our team of six students and four staff arrived in Albania at the end of March; just five months after the country had opened. Again, we found ourselves among the first to enter a country at a significant time in history. A women, I'll call Lisa sent us the invitation by e-mail, met us at the airport and took us to the capital city of Tirana.

Lisa introduced us to Lulietta Pallaveski, nicknamed

Luli, a single mother in her twenties, barely five feet tall with long, straight dark hair. When she smiled, you noticed a single gold tooth she was quite proud of. Luli had spunk and determination. She spoke English so we hired her as a translator for our medical team. This was a good fit as she was also a nurse.

It was unusual to be a single mother in Albania in the early nineties. If a girl found herself with an unwanted pregnancy, the government paid for and encouraged abortion. This was usually the choice. Luli was a woman of principle and able to stand against the public opinion of her time. She was regarded as a second-class citizen for her choice to keep the pregnancy and her baby.

Lueiada was now four, soon to be five. She looked like a younger version of her mother. They lived with Luli's parents who provided daycare while she worked days at the Tirana University Hospital. She didn't know Christ but seemed to have a high ideals and values.

Our team formed an instant bond with her when we first met at the Tirana Hotel. She arranged for us to rent small apartments owned by some of her relatives, where our team could live for the two weeks we would be staying in the capital. When we moved the team to Velora, a city in the south, she arranged for us to stay at the home of other relatives living there. This also provided the host family with much needed extra income.

The countryside was peppered with gray concrete

domes the size of small houses. They were in yards, in front of shops, everywhere, as far as the eye could see, more domes. One day Doug asked, "What are all those concrete domes?"

"Oh, those are bunkers," said Lulie, "To protect us against the imperialist Americans."

"Did you really think we would attack?" Doug quizzed.

"We were told Americans were evil imperialists. We were frightened of what you might do to us. We built these bunkers as protection in case you bombed us!" The myriad of bunkers surfacing through the bleak, gray skies were a visible reminder of the oppressive atmosphere over the country. Darkness never seemed so dark. Could we really bring the light of Jesus to this land?

Songs of Remembrance – "Love Me Tender"

A government official was sent to help us relocate from the capital city, to the city Vlora, in a region south in the country. We were surprised he spoke English.

"How did you learn English so well?" queried Doug.

"As a young boy while listening to Radio Free Europe, I sang along with all the Elvis songs. Soon I had the words memorized but didn't know what they meant. I found an English dictionary and looked up the words. I know every Elvis song ever played on the radio. That's how I learned English!"

Doug couldn't resist this chance for fun! "Can we sing together?" Doug quipped. For the duration of the long car trip they crooned, "Love Me Tender," "You Ain't Nothin' but a Hound Dog," "Blue Suede Shoes," and any other Elvis songs they could remember

Who would have thought he'd be singing Elvis songs in Albania? Doug was having the time of his life. He hardly noticed the car's lack of shocks on the bumpy ride. His medical practice hadn't been nearly this much fun. God used that man to "love Doug tender."

Easter Resurrected After 50 Years

With atheism the state religion, I couldn't imagine that we would have any kind of Easter celebration that year. A week later, three of us from the team were invited to Sunday dinner at the home of a high official, I'll call Surgo. We didn't know what to expect. Dressed in our finest we stood at the door of his home waiting for someone to answer the doorbell. The official's son answered the ring. He would be our translator for the day. Once inside we realized we had been invited to Easter dinner!

This Sunday was Easter in the Greek Orthodox tradition, a week later than when we celebrate. Surgo, said he and his wife had been raised Orthodox. The family practiced their faith before Communism took over. Little did we know the memory of this day would be forever burned in our hearts!

"We are so honored to have you here,"Surgo said. We knew he meant it; his eyes danced as he spoke.

"Please sit down. They had gone to great lengths and expense to provide an elegant meal for us. His wife had prepared the traditional Easter meal as she remembered it as a child. We were in awe. Who would have thought there would be Easter in Albania? Just think, we were privileged to be there experiencing it!

"What a beautiful table," said Janet, one of our team.

In the center of the table was a big round loaf of bead with a cross baked on the top. A red egg was baked into the center of the cross.

"Surgo does this bread have some meaning?" asked Doug.

"I will explain to you our tradition." Surgo took the bread in his hands and blessed it. He broke it apart and took out the egg. "This is Jesus coming out of the tomb. The bread is His body. The red egg symbolizes His blood given for you."

We didn't know anyone in Albania even knew about communion. Yet, his words sounded as those of Jesus at the Last Supper. We all ate a piece of the bread. Doug looked at me, I looked at our friend Janet, with tears in my eyes, the magnitude and significance of this astounding historical event was sinking into our souls. I wondered if the others were feeling the same lump in their heart as I was.

The 56-year-old continued, "I was six when I last celebrated Easter. Now, we are allowed once again to practice our faith. It is such an honor for me to have you here today to be with our family at such a special time."

"Surgo, we are the ones who are honored to be with you," said Doug struggling to talk beyond the lump in his throat.

At that, Surgo suddenly got up from his chair. "Let me show you something." He left the room and returned from the bedroom with a picture with many creases. The colors were faded but we could tell who it was. He had pulled out an old tattered picture of Christ.

"Where did you get that?" Doug asked, hardly able to talk by now.

"I have kept this between my mattress and the springs of my bed for the last 50 years. It was too risky to talk about Him to my children. I didn't share about Him with them. You know how children talk. I was afraid if they found out I would be shot like many others were. I kept my faith in Jesus hidden in my heart and under the mattress." Tears welled up in our eyes.

"I want to tell you how much of an honor it is for me to have you with me and my family as we celebrate our first Easter in 50 years. I just hope I remembered everything right from my childhood. Thank you, thank you for celebrating the resurrection of our Lord with us." With that, the tears flowed freely down all of our faces.

"Surgo, we are the ones who are privileged today. Thank you for letting us share this very special day with you," said Doug.

Surgo went on, while his son translated, to explain the significance of the other memorable things we were eating. Our memories though of that Easter were not of a great meal, but of the treasure hidden in darkness that came to light.

Many times I am reminded that if Doug and I hadn't answered the call of God when we did, we would have missed this day. Wow! We got to be a part of history in the making. We experienced the day Easter was resurrected in Albania.

A Remnant Remains

It looked like a castle with a high stone wall surrounding it, with huge heavy looking double wooden doors with a chain across them. Luli, our Albanian translator, got out of our van and pulled on the thick rope hanging next to the door. Soon the door opened. A monk dressed in a long brown robe with a rope tied around his waist stood in the opening. We were at a monastery. Luli and the monk chatted in Albanian. A few minutes later Luli yelled to us in the van, "It's all right to come in."

We followed the monk to the chapel in the compound. The monastery had been built in the 12th century. The chapel had beautiful paintings of Christ and His disciples depicting various stories in the Bible. The paint was faded and cracked but the beauty was breathtaking.

"How long have you been living in this place? Doug asked.

"This monastery has been here for centuries." We stood in amazement, as Luli translated the remarkable story.

"A few years after the Communists took over our country, the soldiers finally came here. We had heard all forms of religion were banned. There were stories of putting priests in barrels in the sea, then shooting the barrels full of holes till they sank."

This made our hearts sink. He continued, "During our church service, soldiers banged on our door and barged into the chapel."

"Get out. You will no longer worship your God here. You all must come with us." They started waving their guns. The monk waved his arms to demonstrate this terrifying action.

"We knew we would probably be killed. Our leader asked if we could celebrate Holy Communion first before leaving with them.

"Oh all right, but hurry," said the soldiers.

"They stood by and watched as we served Holy

Communion to each other. We were sure it would be our last. Then a miracle happened. The head soldier came up to us and whispered, 'Just stay in this compound. You must never come out or we will have to kill you.' Then, they all left. That was nearly 50 years ago. We are self-contained here, so it wasn't hard to do as they said. God preserved this place and us. It was a miracle."

We felt like we were standing on Holy Ground! Moreover, to think, these were the very monks who thought they were having their last communion. It is one thing to hear of a miracle, it is another thing to see the fruit of one. We stood in awe at what God had done here. This was indeed a special place.

The monk then asked us if we wanted to see the tower and the view from the top. We hated to leave the chapel but wanted to be good guests so we went. Just before I climbed the stairs, I asked him, "Do you have the Bible in Albanian?"

"Is there such a thing?" he replied. "No, I only have it in Greek." I reached into my backpack and pulled out one of the many Bibles that I always carried and handed him one.

The view from the top of the tower was spectacular but not as great as the one in the chapel. When I descended to the bottom of the stairs, many monks all in their long brown robes were lined up waiting for us. My heart went out to them who had endured so much.

"Please, please do you have more Bibles? Could we each have one?" I reached into my backpack and gave them all I had.

I wanted to crawl into the now-empty backpack and cry. I was so overcome with the thought that God had taken me, a nobody, from a small town in northern Michigan and used me to give His precious Word to His anointed ones, to these beautiful saints who had suffered so much. They could read the Word of God in their own language.

The enormity of it sank in. I thought *what if we hadn't left our old lives in Michigan when we did? We wouldn't be here experiencing this awesome privilege.*

Friendship Evangelism

Not only were we able to make a difference with those we met, but it turns out we had a profound influence on those closest to us. We needed more translators for the clinics, ones who understood medicine. Patriot Hojah spoke English, and was in his last year of medical school. We put in a request to the chief of staff at the local hospital, asking for Patriot to help us. Patriot was happy to be relieved of his studies to work with the foreign doctors.

"I am so happy to meet you, Dr. Doug," said Patroit. "I want to learn from you. I want you to teach me to be a really fine doctor!" Patroit was happy to be exposed to the western way. He was searching for the meaning of life. It seems God had handpicked him for us also.

These two precious people Patroit and Luli, our

translators, worked alongside us daily in the medical clinics. They would eat dinner with us, and spend evenings with us before returning to their own places for the night.

As a way to unwind from the day, we always planned a fun activity in the evening. I had brought Bob Fitts's tape, *Highest Place* with me. Patriot's favorite was the song. "*Glory, glory Lord.*" We would put it on full blast and dance around just praising God. Patroit and Luli were totally caught up in all the excitement and fun we were having.

On Lueiada's fifth birthday, we held a huge party for her where we lavished gifts on her from her 'auntie's and uncles.' She had never had a birthday cake before. I had brought cake mixes with us from the US to use for parties. We had to make an appointment at an oven down the street, and then carry the freshly mixed cake two blocks to get it baked! What a delight this was for her when she saw the cake and candles. Her eyes lit up with wonder as we sang, "*Happy Birthday to you.*" I'm not sure who was more blessed that day.

"How can you have so much fun and not be drinking Rockie (Albanian vodka)?" inquired Patriot. He started asking questions about our God. Doug got them each a Bible and we would sit at night and introduce them to Jesus. Patroit hungered so much for things of God that he read through the whole Albanian New Testament in his free time. The women mostly worked with Luli answering her questions about God. Following this intensive one on one, they each came to the point where they prayed asking Jesus into their heart. There was no holding them back now. They begged for communion and to be baptized.

"The body of Christ given for you," said Doug as he served them communion for the first time. There were no churches or people to disciple them. We would need to do the best we could while here and ask God to take care of them when we left.

"Could we take you to a special place in the forest, we will roast a 'lamb cooked in hell' (roasted on a spit). It will be fun, you will enjoy this," said one of the physicians at the local hospital in the town we were staying. Luli and Patroit had a plan. This forest was on the way to the Ionian Sea. "Would you please baptize us?" pleaded Patroit to Doug. Since there wasn't a church or a pastor available to do this, Doug agreed.

We left the physicians turning the lamb on the spit and consuming Rockie almost as quickly as the spit was turning. They hardly noticed when we left. It was a beautiful drive down the mountain to the sea. The water and mountains looked almost like heaven. When we got to the sea, Doug read the account where Jesus commanded us to be baptized. Luli was first. Standing in the water with them, Doug totally immersed her symbolizing the old man dying and the new man coming forth. Luli came up out of the water ecstatic with joy, so delighted to be in God's family. Patroit came up shouting praises to God.

Patroit and Luli were noticeably different after that day at the sea. They seemed to radiate an inner peace, which carried on into the medical clinics as well.

What's His Name?

What's in a name? Doug was soon to answer that question in a way he never expected! We had been running medical clinics for weeks in the small villages around Velora treating 50 to 60 patients each day. The free medical care and medicine was definitely a draw. We had to try to keep the long lines moving in order to see everyone before dark.

It was getting late when a woman about 45 years old had her turn to see Dr. Doug. He noticed that she looked older than her years. Life is hard for women in Albania. The women do all the cooking, laundry, childcare, and work in the fields.

Her complaints seemed vague. Finally, to save time Doug asked impatiently, "What's really going on? Why are you really here?"

She dropped her head. After a long pause she stammered, "I ... I ... know somebody made all this," pointing to the sky and moving her arm around in a circle. I've been talking to Him in the fields all these years. But... but... what's His name? I heard that you people know His name."

Tears came to Doug's eyes. He let out a big sigh. He hadn't expected to hear this reply.

"Let me tell you about God and His son Jesus..." he

began.   Forget the schedule.   If this woman could spend 45 years talking to God, he could spend the time it took to introduce her to Him!   That woman left knowing not only God's name but knowing she would spend eternity with Him.   Somehow, all the patients were seen that day.

For Doug and I all these incredible experiences made us glad we hadn't waited to go into missions.   Doug once said, "Money can't buy all the experiences that we've had."   That day he truly got to "reap where he did not sow."   The prayers of the saints had gone before us to this darkened place, this almost-Hell.

Light came not only to Albania, but also to our hearts. We had made the right choice in leaving home.   We had answered "the call."

Chapter 6

TRAVELING OUR NEW PATH:
Comfortable in Our Calling

*"Trust in the Lord... and He will show you which
path to take (Prov.3:5, 6) (NLT)*

A New Path

"How do we find a way to use our profession to serve
the Lord?" Doug would often ask. We just wanted to use
what we knew, medicine. We could go to a foreign field
and make a difference using our skills but that would only
touch a few. We wanted to go further, to multiply ourselves,
to challenge others to take what they already knew and
apply it in a developing nation where the needs were great

and the resources few. Doug had a purpose, a dream, a vision. He wasn't satisfied until he could find a way to help other medical professionals get involved in cross-cultural mission work.

One day he blurted out a thought. "Let's start a class to teach medical people how to minister in developing nations." We had already worked with non-professionals without previous medical training. Our heart was also to teach professionals how to integrate practicing medicine and sharing the Gospel.

Doug approached the Director of the Kona Crossroads Discipleship Training School (CDTS), the same course we had taken back in 1991, with this idea.

"What do you think about combining the curriculum of the CDTS with some training for medical professionals on how to practice medicine in developing nations?" Doug asked. He went on to explain. "I know when I focus only on the needs while practicing medicine; I get burned out, as the needs are constant and crushing. One must see medicine as a ministry, incorporate prayer and offer each a chance to receive Christ or else we are just running clinics.

We want to help medical people learn how to minister medically and spiritually, so they are helping body, soul, and spirit. When I am seeing patients and am able to lead them to Christ, I get energized and the day's work doesn't seem so heavy"

"Go for it," the director said enthusiastically. "This

sounds great! Just keep in mind we need to leave the core curriculum intact."

With the "green light," Doug began to develop a hybrid course that would train medical professionals. We found through experience, out in a tent with a dirt floor, one must learn how to function in a medical system with no labs, MRI's, X-rays, or EKG's to assist in making a diagnosis.

We now needed to rely on checking mucus membranes of the eyes to gage anemia, checking the pulse with a different focus to catch arrhythmias, and rely on lung sounds in lieu of x-rays. This can be a very difficult concept to accept when first exposed to medical missions. We already knew how the novice could function on the field; we wanted to teach the world of medical professionals – MDs, RNs, Lab Techs and others.

We led our first Crossroads school with a medical emphasis in April 1994. This class was an exceptional class with many skills and professions represented not just medicine. They would all need to learn how to incorporate "what they knew" into the world of missions.

Doug recruited Dr. Peter Murphy, one of our former students to teach classes for the medical section. Once a week, for 12 weeks, we separated the 13 medical professionals from the rest of the class for special sessions on "missionary medicine." At the end of 12 weeks, the whole class was ready. All 51 students would be going for their practicum into uncharted territory.

A New Ministry

Once again, we found ourselves in a formerly closed country, this time in Ukraine, part of the former Soviet Union. With the fall of the Berlin Wall, this country began to open up. It was almost like going back into a time warp. The buildings were old with the paint absent or peeling off. The streets were badly in need of repair; however, this didn't seem to be a problem as we saw very few cars. All the women wore skirts and the women over 50 years of age wore babushkas on their heads. Big old trucks were on many corners selling freshly baked bread from the back.

Two weeks before our arrival, a small team had come from Oregon to start YWAM in Ternopil. We joined them with our class of 90 people – 51 students, their children, and a few staff, ranging in ages from eight months to seventy-four years! We took this diverse group half way around the world from Hawaii for an eight-week practicum. This was quite an undertaking for us, quite different from the small teams we were used to leading.

We divided the class into three teams, each going to a different part of the country. Each team had a different focus: medical work, evangelistic work, and ministry to business people. Deb, from Oregon, was fluent in Ukrainian and had arranged for translators to be with each of the teams.

Since our mission usually tries to work alongside the local church, we arranged for each team to partner with a local church. There weren't many churches yet as most had been closed down under Communist rule. The medical team went to the Ternopil area; the business team, made up of former business professionals, to Odessa, a city in the southern area on the Black Sea; and an evangelistic team went to Kharkov in the northeastern region.

Using Business for Missions

Each group of students is unique. Along with the medical people we had recruited, we had several very successful businessmen in this class. Doug had another idea brewing. His mind was always very fertile.

"Bobby, I'd like you and Jean to be the student leaders of a team of business people. Your assignment is to make contact with the business community in Odessa and show them how to apply biblical principles to running a business." Bobby had run several successful businesses before coming to Crossroads so he was the perfect choice to give leadership to this team.

Six weeks after arriving in the country, we received a call from Bobby. "We have a business seminar scheduled for next Thursday. Would you like to come down to Odessa and attend it? You can get a feel for what we are doing here."

"You can count on us to be there," answered Doug. We

took the overnight train and arrived a few days before the big event in order to see what other ministries this team was doing in addition to the seminar. We wanted to see it all.

The day for the seminar arrived. We crowded into a 12' x 12' room packed with people dressed in business attire, TV cameramen, radio interviewers and all their equipment, in addition to our students. Bobby shared business principles from the Bible such as: a worker is worthy of a fair wage; keep your word, even when it hurts; don't accept bribes (commonplace for many of them).

We would have stayed until the end of their presentation but had to catch a train back to Ternopil early that afternoon. Though we missed the final bit, we left with a sense of joy and pride, seeing how well the students on this team had adapted to the culture, made friends with the locals and were now making a difference.

When all our teams got back together for the debriefing time at the end of the outreach, Bobby couldn't wait to show us a newspaper article reporting on the seminar. He could hardly contain his laughter. In Ukrainian culture, acknowledging the leader is very important. Bobby had the article translated, and gleefully read his favorite line which described the "head chief" (Doug).

The article said, "An elderly gentleman with a gray mustache had to leave early to catch a train…." Bobby was only one year younger than Doug, and this comment delighted him no end. "The elderly gentleman with the gray mustache," Bobby repeated, howling once again, and patting Doug on the shoulder. Doug just rolled his eyes.

"Notice anything different?" Doug said as he came out of the bathroom the next morning. The mustache he had sported for 20 years was conspicuously missing! Bobby never let him forget that incident. It was all part of the fun of being in a new culture and getting a new perspective on a whole lot of things, including ourselves.

Country Connections

Keeping your sense of humor on the mission field is essential, but missions also have many serious moments. One such moment that touched us personally happened on our visit to the evangelistic team, the only team we had in Eastern Ukraine, the Russian speaking part of the country. We had a chance to try yet another language, though we barely knew any Ukrainian.

This was a very musically talented team. Music crosses all cultures and is a great tool to use for missions. The leader of this team was a former opera singer from London, England. One family on the team was gifted musically, especially one of their daughters; some were painters and carpenters but all liked to sing. We weren't surprised when the church they worked with was very musically oriented. One Sunday we visited that church. We recognized the tunes of many of the songs, the same ones we sang in our churches in the USA. The only difference was that the words were in Russian.

I noticed a keyboard and a great sound system in the

rented auditorium. *Nice equipment*, I thought to myself. I didn't give a thought to where it might have come from. The pastor began his message; I was a bit surprised that he spoke English and the message was translated into Russian, rather than vice-versa. It seems many foreign dignitaries attend this church. The English must have been for them. After the service, our team took us forward to meet the pastor.

"Where are you from in the States?" he asked in perfect English.

"Michigan," answered Doug.

"Traverse City, Michigan?" he queried.

"Traverse City!" Doug exclaimed. "That's only an hour's drive from our home in Michigan."

"Do you know Mike Davis?" the pastor asked.

"I have met him but don't know him well. He came to our church with his team to lead worship for our mission's conference. How do you know him?" Doug asked.

"Mr. Davis and his team helped start this church. They came to our city to start a church, and then left this keyboard and sound system for us."

At this point I looked at Doug through tears in my eyes; I noticed he could hardly speak. We couldn't believe our ears. Four years earlier when Mike and his worship team had been at our church in Michigan, they were getting ready to leave for the former Soviet Union. They took an offering at that service for instruments and sound equipment to leave behind, to bless the church they hoped to pioneer. Doug and I were so touched by this gesture of kindness we gave them a donation.

Now, here we were, halfway around the world seeing the benefits of our own offering. Whew! The goodness of God! How many people actually get to see the fruit of their giving in such a dramatic way? We were praising God, halfway around the world, accompanied by instruments our home church had helped to buy.

Again, I made a mental note; "*We never would have seen any of this – if we hadn't left the comforts of Michigan*".

We Fix Anything

God can use all of His people! You don't have to be famous, have a huge talent, or be a professional., as many would think.

In Kona, before leaving for the Ukraine, Doug announced the names of students on each team. We always pray and ask God who should be on each team. We announced the medical team last. One of our students, J.W. Clayton, didn't hear his name until we announced the medical team members. He came to us later.

"There must be some mistake," he said, a little quizzically. "I'm a mechanic, and you put me on the medical team."

"It's no mistake," said Doug. "I prayed about it, and you are to be on the medical team." J.W. heaved a sigh, didn't object, and just walked away. I knew from experience that Doug must have heard God's voice, but secretly wondered if he was off on this one! But God however, knew what He was doing all along.

J.W.'s Special Assignment

The medical clinic was humming along in the city of Ternopil, Ukraine. In a few weeks, we would take the clinics to the countryside, but today, we were using some rooms in a medical clinic in the city center. Inside, it was orderly but outside the clinic door, patients pushed, shoved, and pleaded to be seen by the doctors from the West. Once inside though, each patient was put into a cubicle, screened off by a curtain.

In this instance, the MD saw the patient first, then directed them to a table where people were waiting to pray with them. We shared the Gospel with each patient and gave him or her, an opportunity to pray to receive Christ. If they did, we gave their names to a local church for follow-up. At the very least, we offered to pray with them, and offered a free Ukrainian Bible, all before they received their free medicine. Few refused prayer or the Bible; all took the free medicine and many received Christ.

In the midst of all this activity, Dr. Oleg came into the clinic looking for Doug. "Do you have anyone who knows how to put an ambulance together? We just received an American ambulance in a container but no one here knows how to put it together!"

J.W. was at a prayer station. "J.W. come here please," said Doug. "There's someone I'd like you to meet…"

J.W. was like a kid in a candy store. For the remainder of our time there, he worked downtown at a garage with other mechanics instructing them on how to put the ambulance together. He talked about Jesus as he worked. He invited many to a Bible study we had in the evening for those who wanted to know more about Christ. I don't recall if any accepted the Lord but I do know he reached a segment of society that we didn't reach at the clinic. Once again confirming, we are all needed regardless of our education or skills. Doug had heard God back in Kona when praying about the teams. Indeed, J.W., "the mechanic", was to be on the medical team. The medical community really needed his expertise. God uses whatever talent we offer Him, we just need to offer it!

Jews Sharing Jesus

Some of our students called themselves "completed Jews." They converted to Christ from a Jewish background. It has been a privilege watching many of these students. Some continued to celebrate the Jewish holidays and would invite us to share in the same feasts Jesus observed, helping us all to experience a greater richness in our understanding of our Lord.

Many of these same students also have a heart to reach out to other Jewish people with the news of the Messiah. Such was the case in Ukraine. The Jews have suffered a great deal of persecution there and even mass executions. The ones who remain appear to be suspicious of anyone who is not Jewish.

"I want to find out if there are any Jews remaining in this city," said Dusty, one of our Crossroads students.   A Jew herself, she found a small monument on a wall in the inner city, honoring those who were slaughtered there. Near it was a flyer announcing a Jewish service coming up on Friday at 5 p.m. She went to the service but didn't reveal she was with a Christian mission organization. She went back week after week developing a friendship with them. It came to her attention that there was an old rundown Jewish cemetery nearby. "Would you take me there?" she asked her new friend.

It was hardly distinguishable as a cemetery. Weeds had grown up so tall, the headstones were barely visible. "I had to wade through high weeds and prickly brush to follow my host to a grave he wanted me to see," Dusty later recalled.

"This is the grave of my great Uncle. He was one of those executed in the city square," said her host. "It is a shame his grave is hidden, along with all the others; it seems nobody knows or cares, that he ever lived." She could see that the task of cleaning it up would be as hopeless as they felt.

Dusty had an idea, and it led to some action. The following Saturday, on their day off, the entire medical team showed up at that cemetery. The men and children pulled weeds. The women went to the outdoor market to buy flowers and flower seeds.

By late afternoon, the cemetery looked like a place of honor for the people buried there. Dusty and the team had demonstrated in a practical way the love of Jesus, by honoring those of another faith. When her Jewish friends first saw the now-clean cemetery, some cried, some laughed as they ran around the headstones, looking for the names of relatives.

"Why would you do this for us?" asked her Jewish friend.

"Let me tell you about. . . ."

What a privilege to extend love instead of hate to God's chosen people. The cemetery has become more beautiful over the years. This team left more then medical help in Ukraine; they left the handprint of God, and in the process left hope restored. This team didn't limit themselves--it seems they could fix anything.

God Can Fix the Brokenhearted

We were holding an afternoon clinic in downtown Ternopil. The large room was abuzz with people. Nurses were taking histories and physicals; patients were being seen by the doctors; others were being prayed for by a prayer team. I was working the pharmacy. A lady in her mid-fifties dressed in all black with a black veil on her head walked in to Doug's station to be seen by him.

I overheard them talking, "Doctor I have been in constant pain since my husband died two years ago," she said through a translator.

"Where are you having pain?" Doug asked.

"In all my joints, I ache in all my joints," she repeated as she rubbed her wrist.

Doug examined her but didn't find anything obvious that would be causing her pain. Then he had an idea. "You say your husband died two years ago?"

"Yes, and ever since then I have been hurting all over," she said continuing to rub her wrist.

"May we pray for you? I am going to ask Jesus to take away your pain. I think your pain is in your soul rather then your body. Pam, the nurse, and I will pray for you right now if that is okay with you," he said.

After the prayer Doug noticed her face lit up, and she said she felt better. God touched her and pulled her out of her deep grief. They invited her to come to a Bible study that night to learn more about Jesus. She came bringing her 12-year-old son with her. Pam almost didn't recognize her. Gone was all the black widow's attire. She had bright colored clothes on and a huge smile on her face. She proudly announced all her pain was gone. They continued to come back week after week. Her face got more radiant. Her son related to the young kids on the team. They both received the healing they needed from the only One who could heal their grief – Jesus.

And to think God was using us, from a small town in Northern Michigan to bring His healing to His precious hurting children half a world away from us. What if we had not come? I get teary thinking about it. All of our lives would be so much poorer.

I Want To Go To the Mountains

We returned to Ukraine for three more summers after our first trip. We had many more experiences equally as profound in those following years. From the very first year, however, Doug had a desire go to the gypsy camps.

"I hear that the Gypsies in the Carpathian Mountains are an unreached people group. Can you arrange for us to take a team there?" Doug begged Deb as they discussed various ministry needs and opportunities. On our last trip to Ukraine, his dream came true. In this class was Dr. Craig Wendt, a general surgeon and friend from our hometown of Petoskey, Michigan. Craig had come with his wife, Pat and four children to take our special medical Crossroads class. We knew him and his family well.

Deb had made plans to take a small medical team to the

mountains. Since Doug knew Craig's oldest daughter Katie was interested in medicine, he invited her to accompany the team. We felt it was very important to involve the children of our students in the ministry. God calls families. They are not just along for the ride, but we consider them a vital link in ministry. Many times the children open doors for us. People love watching them minister. Doug asked Katie, then 14, to lead worship for the small group going to the mountains.

"I don't think I can," sighed Katie, as she gazed at the ground.

"I know you can," said Doug. Katie finally agreed but not without a lot of encouragement. She was the youngest on the mountain team. The rest were all professionals. She told us later, she wondered, *what do I have to offer? I'm only 14.* But Katie took her assignment seriously. She knew the value of starting each day with worship and earnestly sought the Lord for the correct songs. She found she enjoyed this assignment and discovered Doug was right! She became a missionary on that trip.

Katie is grown now. She served in YWAM, in England, where she met her husband. She put medicine on hold. It's amazing how her parents willingness to explore missions as a second career, had changed the course of this young women's life. Sometimes, we never know what fruit will come from our obedience in answering "the call."

Doug loved being "out there" with the people, whether it was in Guyana, Albania, Ukraine, or other nations. He enjoyed pioneering new things in new places. He didn't expect, though that he would soon be asked to do something that would lead us into a whole new phase of ministry.

New Responsibilities: Becoming a Dean

"Would you pray about accepting the position of Dean of the College of Counseling and Health Care for the Kona campus?", a University of the Nations leader asked Doug. He was in the midst of running yet another medical CDTS.

"Oh, all right," said Doug, as he heaved a sigh. He was tired of hearing this request. Many thought he was wasting his time leading an entry-level discipleship and mission's course.

"As a doctor," they would say, "You should be working with the health care training programs." Doug reluctantly agreed to pray about it, just to get them off his back.

Our longtime friend, Janet Ditto, had given leadership to the College of Counseling and Health Care (CCHC) for 10 years, but now, was preparing to leave. Doug, always a visionary, was starting to feel restless. Maybe this was the answer. The medical CDTS was well established, and he needed a new challenge. Merely maintaining what he had started was not life giving to Doug. Remembering the words of Jesus that He had come to bring us life, Doug decided it wouldn't hurt to pray about the request. Maybe it was the Lord's idea, though at the time it didn't appeal much to Doug.

The new position would require us to live in Kona year round and that was a concern we had. With our current position, we would be away eight months and home four, allowing us to return every fall to our cabin in Michigan. The fall was Doug's favorite time of the year. He loved the hunting season. We decided that if he took this position he would continue to return to Michigan every deer-hunting season. The male bonding time with my father and our sons was something he didn't want to miss.

Another consideration was that my parents, our daughter, and grandchild lived in Michigan. The writer, Oswald Chambers says, "Our obedience to God sometimes costs others." I knew my parents would want us to follow the call of God, yet my mother needs extra assistance with her care, and I would often help my father with her when I could. This would mean I wouldn't be able to relieve him as often.

The thought of being long-distance grandparents was the hardest thing to consider. I had previously written my granddaughter a letter when she was only seven months old, explaining why we weren't around more in her life. I put the letter in the safe, and asked her mother to give it to her, if something should happen to us. The cost was indeed high. Once again we needed direction and confirmation from the Lord. We counted the cost of this next phase, but we knew that what was needed was hearing clearly from the Lord.

Over the next several weeks, we prayed and sought the Lord together for His direction. One day Doug blurted out with a sigh, "Jan, I think God wants me to take the Dean position." I concurred. I had sensed the same thing. At this point we were choosing to be obedient to God even though this wasn't necessarily the desire of our hearts. The life we had become accustomed to in the past few years would have to be laid on the altar in order to follow the call of God in this next phase.

Recalling the words given to us years ago before we started this new journey, we prayed together through our tears, asking God, "to take care of our lambs as we took care of His sheep!" Knowing the importance of hearing the voice of God concerning a life-changing decision, we had asked for and received scriptural confirmation. It was the Lord who was asking Doug to become Dean, not the need of the ministry.

Shortly thereafter, Doug's acceptance of this new role was made public at a campus staff meeting in Kona. People cheered! In the fall of 1997, after we had completed our last outreach to the Ukraine, Doug was installed as the Dean of the College of Counseling and Health Care at the University of the Nations, Kona. We returned to Michigan to prepare for living in Kona full time. He began his duties on campus the following January, a month of new beginnings, just a month before the dedication of the new health care building.

Doug's duties included giving oversight to numerous classes in both the Health Care, Counseling, and Family

Ministry departments of the college. The post had been vacant for some time so the first task would be to gather information. What did this college look like now? Then we would seek God and see what He wanted it to look like!

Doug believed very strongly in having an open door to his staff, and gave the staff ownership in the various changes to be made in the college. God had put the disenfranchised children of the world on his heart way back in Guyana. The HIV/AIDS epidemic was also dear to his heart. He began to ask God what he could do in this new position to help. How could we as believers in Christ help those who desperately need to know Him and His touch?

The desires of Doug's heart began to change as he dug more into this new position as the Dean. He was finding he really enjoyed building this department. What began as obedience was now becoming fun and bringing him life rather than dragging him down.

Again, I reflected, *what if we had waited until retirement*? Doug was truly positioned to affect change in many parts of the world. The purposes of God were greater than either of us could see. After being in this position for four years, Doug would take another pathway – not of his choosing.

Chapter 7

ROCKS IN THE PATH:

Our Greatest Challenge

"Blessed is the man who perseveres under trial, he will receive the crown of life that God has promised to those who love Him" (James 1:12).

Something is Wrong!

"Something is terribly wrong," the voice said on the other end of the phone.

We all dread receiving the phone call I received. A call can change your life forever – like it did mine.

"Doug is acting strangely. We think he needs a checkup." It was Lin Yi, one of our students calling from Tulsa, Oklahoma where he was doing his practicum for the Introduction to Children Social Services class. Doug, had co-authored the class curriculum, and had gone to Tulsa to observe. The phone had abruptly interrupted my sleep. It was only 5:15 a.m., still dark on this early January morning in Hawaii. *Was this a bad dream?*

Since Doug had left on Tuesday for Tulsa, my week had been full of worries about him. Before he left, he seemed somewhat confused and more forgetful. He always needed to bring a task to completion, or he was out of sorts. However, this time it was different.

"Jan, I really shouldn't be going. I have so much left to do in my office," he said as we were leaving his office for the plane. I felt a twinge. He had been working too hard. It was just a few weeks ago, at the beginning of the New Year that I had asked him not to go in to work anymore on weekends. For the past six months, he had been coming in one full day each weekend to "catch up."

"Doug, you need a break from this place. You're here too much." I said.

He promised that in the New Year, he wouldn't come in on weekends. Looking around his office at the clutter, I could see he did have a lot of unfinished work. *Was I responsible for his scattered mess by asking him not to work weekends?* Yet, there were the repeated questions he kept asking….

The previous Saturday evening, we had our whole department from the College of Counseling and Health Care over for a barbecue, nearly 60 people. Doug did the grilling and seemed fine. Yet on Monday, he had repeatedly asked me what time we had to leave for the school's graduation dinner. Was he so busy that he really couldn't remember what I had just told him? Tuesday was the same. "What time does my plane leave?" he must have asked me this question a dozen times. I even asked him once if he was all right.

After he left Kona for Tulsa, I talked to his good friends and colleagues Bobby Norment and Asher Motola. I sat in Bobby's office sharing my concerns. "He's either getting ready to have a nervous breakdown, or he has a brain tumor."

Bobby recalled, "That's funny, on Sunday as he was driving home from golf I asked him to drop me off at Costco where I had left my car. He didn't remember where Costco was. I thought that was strange." We decided that I should call Tulsa to see how he was doing.

R-r-ring. "You have reached the Little Light House. We are sorry but we are closed due to inclement weather," said the answer machine. Tulsa was in a snowstorm. It was enough snow to stop all the normal daily activity. I tried email. No one responded. I had no other way to reach anyone to inquire about him. I tried for days and couldn't get a response.

Four days after that first phone call to Tulsa, I received

a call from Lin Yi, in Tulsa, telling me there was something wrong. My heart dropped to my stomach. The people in Tulsa were seeing something too.

"What are you seeing?" I asked.

"Doug seems confused and he can't remember things. I think you need to talk with Marsha." Marsha Mitchell was the director of Little Light House, the ministry he was visiting. She and her husband had been to our home in Hawaii for dinner a few months ago.

I was fully awake now as I wrote down the phone number. After a phone call to her confirming what Lin Yi had said, I decided to talk with Doug directly. He was staying in a dorm so this took a little bit of work to get through to him. Finally we connected.

"Hi honey. How's it going?" I asked, trying to keep my composure.

"Jan, it's very confusing here. They had a snowstorm and everything is cancelled. They keep changing the schedule on me. It's very frustrating."

"Doug, I think there is more going on here. I talked with Asher and Bobby. We have noticed you are forgetting things."

"Like what?"

"Bobby said you forgot how to get to Costco on Sunday. You forgot the time we were to go to the Gradation dinner on

Monday and you repeatedly asked me what time your plane left on Tuesday. Doug, you seem to be forgetting things."

"Like what? Give me an example."

"Doug, I just did."

Silence.

I spoke again, "Doug people in Tulsa are concerned for you. They think you need a check-up."

More silence.

Then he spoke, "Well, OK, but I want to go back to Petoskey to see Spike (a nickname for his Internist and friend, Dr. Diedrick).

"Tell you what. I'll come to Tulsa, and we'll go home to Michigan together, okay?

"Okay," he agreed.

"I love you honey."

"I love you too, Jan." Click.

Was he crying? The sniffles seemed to suggest that. *Oh Lord, help us,* I pleaded not quite audibly.

The return call came from Spike's nurse in Michigan: "Dr. Diedrick does not want Doug to get on a plane. He may have a bleeder in his brain. He needs to get checked out in Tulsa."

I called back to Marsha in Tulsa. "Tell Doug that Spike

said to get it checked out there." Marsha felt she could take him to an Internist that day. They had one on their board. Assured that he was in good hands, I asked her to tell Doug I'd get there as soon as I could and began preparing for a trip I hadn't dreamed of taking.

The next few hours were a blur. *Oh God,* I prayed silently as I packed, *let him be O.K. Don't let him have a stroke.*

My friend Jane Berggren came over to be with me. She just sat in the same room while I packed. Somehow, just her being there gave me strength. From the time of the phone call to the time I left the house for the plane, was eight hours. One doesn't get off the island of Hawaii quickly!

As I looked around at all the familiar things in the house, I remember thinking, "Would I ever get back here again?" Then I saw it – a gift certificate Doug had given me for Christmas less than a month ago. "A Pampered Lady Certificate," it said, "Good for a hair-do, facial and manicure." It was signed, "To my beautiful wife from your loving and thoughtful husband, Doug." An ache formed in my heart. He always said that to me. He always called me beautiful!   I didn't know it then but I would never return to this house. I walked out of more than the house that held so many memories of our life together. I walked out of my life as I knew it, never to return.

The Longest Night

I took a short flight to Honolulu, from the Big Island of Hawaii, where we lived and worked with YWAM. There I would catch the big DC-10 to the west coast. I waited for my flight in the World Club, a lounge for Northwest Airlines. *I'll call Marsha on her cell phone. Doug should have heard something by now.*

I reached her easily this time, and she put Doug on the phone. In a hushed voice he said, "Jan, I have a brain tumor." Time stood still. I felt like a bomb had exploded in my heart.

"Oh honey!" I could hardly find my voice to talk. "What did they say?"

"It's not good. It's not in a good spot."

I composed myself. "Doug, it's going to be all right. Everything will be okay." I said, trying to convince myself as much as him. "I'll be there at noon tomorrow. We'll talk then. I love you."

"I love you too," he said weakly.

After I hung up the phone, I just stared at the TV. My husband had a brain tumor! The other people in the club were returning from their vacations in Hawaii, tanned and chatting happily with each other. I was alone, and my husband had a brain tumor. I called Jane on the cell phone. I had to talk to somebody that loved me.

"Get the troops praying," I told her. "Doug has a brain tumor."

I usually sleep on the night flight from Hawaii to the West Coast, but no sleep came this time. My husband, the love of my life, was very sick. I was numb. It was the longest flight I have ever taken; at least it seemed it was. All I could think was, *Doug has a brain tumor! Doug has a brain tumor! Oh God, hold onto me tight – please!*

"To Have and To Hold"

As I got off the plane in Tulsa, there stood Doug, his 6'4" tall frame waiting for me. He looked the same as every other time he had met me at the airport except for the tears that started welling up in his eyes. He hugged me longer than usual, and he took my hand as we walked down the long corridor to get my baggage. We didn't say anything. We didn't have to. When you've been married as long as we have, communication often flows without words.

After lunch and the usual niceties with our hosts, Doug and I were finally alone. Our hosts, the Mitchells, had a lovely glass sun porch they had recently added onto their home.

Everything about it was bright, with many windows and lots of sunlight. Inside, it was toasty. On the other side of all those glass windows were scattered piles of leftover snow from the storm a few days earlier. Music played softly in the background. The Mitchells graciously gave us this little place to be alone, alone and together.

Doug showed me the films from the MRI. He explained, "The tumor is the size of your fist. It crosses over into both ventricles right in the middle of the brain. It is not a good spot. It's right where you live, Jan."   I didn't think it was possible to be any more numb than I was after hearing the news of the brain tumor. Yet, what I was hearing seemed surreal. *Oh God, this can't be happening!*

We hugged each other a lot that day. Sometimes in knowing silence, other times quietly crying. This was the hardest thing we had ever faced. A full gamut of emotions surfaced. At one point he even asked, "Why me Lord? I've served you, left my home, children and grandchild to serve you. Why me? Lord, I have so much I still want to do. There are classes yet to write, ministries to start, a book to write!" "Jan...I don't want to leave you." He started to sob from deep within.

Mostly he sat in the corner chair, tears welling in his eyes, occasionally spilling down his cheeks. With hands raised in the air, he sang along with the music, worshiping. This was so like Doug. He loved to praise God, even at a time like this. I wondered, *Was this the sacrifice of praise?*

We made many phone calls from that room all weekend. We called each of our three children, my parents, Doug's sister, and Dr. Henry Singer back in Petoskey. Henry was Doug's long-time friend. He offered to make an appointment with Dr. Ciluffo early the following week. Maybe Dr. Ciluffo would tell us that the MRI was wrong, that this was all a horrible mistake!

The Mitchell's had a cocker spaniel puppy who reminded us of the one we had left behind when we went into missions work full-time. It seemed she thought it was her duty to love us and sleep with us. Somehow, when she jumped onto our laps and nuzzled us with her nose, we felt loved. We needed to feel all the love we could right then. This dog helped ease the pain we both were feeling. Even in this small way, we felt the Lord bringing comfort in this dark valley.

We spent most of the weekend, except for church and meals, in that sun porch. It took us time to digest the events of the last few days. We would have to wait until Monday morning to catch a flight back to our home in Michigan. Was it only a week ago we'd had a party at our house? What a difference a phone call makes!

There is No Place like Home

Monday morning came. It was time to return to Michigan. The entire Little Light House staff met us at the airport to see us off! Tears flowed. The unspoken was never spoken. Instead, there were hugs and promises of prayer.

Our plane touched down in Detroit on the way to Petoskey. Doug's sister, Joan, met us at the gate. They held each other and tears passed between them. Just six years ago they had lost their mother. Six months later, Joan had lost her husband. Now, was Joan about to lose her only brother?

We arrived in Petoskey a few hours later. Snow covered the ground. It was definitely winter, very different from Hawaii where we had been just a week earlier. Our friends and church had stocked the refrigerator and turned up the heat in the house. We were home.

In times of crisis there is no place like home. This is where Doug wanted to be. This home used to be our "cabin by the lake." But, in 1994, after we sold our big house, we remodeled the cabin and made it into a modest retirement home. Doug had seemed to need this more then I did. He found it comforting to know where his "stuff" was. He called it "field dependency," a need to know where your chain saw, hunting boots, fishing rods, etc. were just in case you wanted them.

The remodeled cabin was the only place we ever lived where he'd sit down, look around and remark. "God, I love this place." It was appropriate that we came back to the home he loved. Another big reason, he trusted the physicians here. He had worked with most of them throughout his 18 years of practice. He knew who was good. So did I, having worked in ICU.

John Ciluffo, a neurosurgeon, was the only one Doug would allow to "cut on his brain."

As we sat quietly in John's office the next morning,

John looked at Doug's MRI.

"Where have you been?" he asked. The tumor looked so strange. At first, Dr. Ciluffo thought it might be TB of the brain, which is treatable. He leveled with us though, not wanting to give us hope that was unfounded. "I don't think it is though. The only way to know for sure is do a biopsy," he said plaintively.

A biopsy is cutting out a piece of the tumor for diagnoses. Doug reluctantly agreed. He seemed to think it wasn't necessary; he had seen the MRI, and there was no doubt about what he saw. For his family's sake, he agreed to the biopsy. I had to know for sure. If he did have something treatable, and we didn't treat it, then I'd never be able to forgive myself. The date of the surgery was set for the following Monday.

Joyful Despite Limitations

On Friday, February 4, 2000 just four days after our appointment with the doctor, the Chancellor of the University of the Nations in Kona, David Boyd, stopped by on his way back to Hawaii from the National Prayer Breakfast in Washington D.C. He had only seven hours to be with us.

Our good friend, Jim Manthei, picked him up and brought him over. Jim's wife, Marlys, and I sat at the table as Doug, Jim, and David sat in the living room tossing around ideas. All three of them were visionaries. It was stimulating, exciting, and entertaining to listen to the three of them talk. Listening to their conversation, one would never know Doug had a problem - unless we had asked him what day it was!

Later, as we sat at the table for lunch, we all were trying to remember someone's name. Doug came up with the answer. David said, "Hey, you're the one with the brain tumor." We all laughed. Doug never forgot a face or a name. He had nearly a photographic memory.

After David left, it was time for our boys to arrive from different parts of the U.S. Our daughter Tamara lived in town, a short distance from our cabin.

"Call them home," Dr. Ciluffo had said. "There is a chance he will never be the same person after surgery. Doug as you know him might not be there."

Doug knew this too, I think. He prayed, "God, please don't let this destroy the faith of my children. Keep them always for You." He prayed this often and earnestly, along with, "Lord, don't let me do or say anything that will not bring honor to you." He used to have a foul mouth, and he was afraid if he wasn't in his right mind, some bad language might spill out. It never did! God answered both of his prayers.

Others Come Alongside

Our home church rallied around him at the Sunday service. That evening, our pastor drove the 60 miles to the hospital in Traverse City where the surgery was scheduled for the next day. Doug rode with pastor in his truck so they could be alone to talk together. The kids and I went separately in the car. I didn't discover what they discussed until much later. Doug was telling Pastor Bill what he wanted said at his funeral. We all stayed overnight at the hospital's hotel for families and patients from out of town.

"For Better or Worse"

The day of the surgery was a long one. Doug was having an MRI at 7:00 a.m. but waited around until 12:00 noon to be taken in for surgery. It wasn't until 7:00 p.m. that night that Dr. Ciluffo called us into a private waiting room.

Dr. Ciluffo is an excellent surgeon. He was also direct and frank with us. I was grateful that our two pastors were with the kids and me in the room.

"It's worse than I thought," he said. "I almost lost him on the table because of bleeding. I couldn't remove any of the tumor as we'd hoped to. It was green mush. We don't have the results of the biopsy yet, but I'm sure the tumor is a grade four malignant astrocytomia – the worst kind. He might have three to nine months left. He won't have much pain but will just get sleepier and sleepier. You'd better pick out a nursing home. He's a big guy. There will come a time that you won't be able to take care of him." I thought I heard a slight quiver in his voice with the next two words. "I'm sorry." There was no time to talk, no time for questions. He had another surgery to do and had to leave.

We all sat in stunned silence. No one said a word. Then one by one, each of us started sobbing. The pastors took turns holding us while each of them sobbed also. We had all been praying for a different report. *God where are you now? Do you even care?*

The next day was a blur. Visiting Doug in ICU, calling family and friends, and coping with this shocking news was all I could do. They moved Doug out of ICU into a regular room. He knew us even though he'd just had a hole drilled through his head. He seemed pretty much the same as before the surgery, but was still groggy from the pain medicine.

R-r-ring. My heart stopped. It was 11 p.m., and I was reading in bed in our hotel room near the hospital. I was just getting ready to go to sleep.

"Mrs. Kinne, this is your husband's nurse. Dr. Kinne keeps asking us if we've seen his bride. We can't keep him in bed. He keeps coming into the hallway looking for you. Could you possibly come over?"

"I'll be right there as soon as I get dressed," I said sleepily.

Walking into his room at the hospital, I said, "Honey, what's the matter? I'm here with you."

"Jan, I didn't know where you were. I thought you'd left me."

"Doug, I would never leave you. Go to sleep now. I'll be right here next to you."

"Just crawl in here next to me so I can hug you. Please . . . . "

"Honey, I can't do that. But I'll be here, right next to you holding your hand." I sat in the recliner chair next to his bed. *Lord, help us. Please help us.*

"Mrs. Kinne," the nurse's voice broke the brief silence. "Since you're going to be spending the night here, would you like a blanket?"

"Thanks," I said softly.

Later we found out it was the pain medicine that was making Doug so agitated. I turned on the tape player next to his bed. The words of a familiar song took on a new meaning that night. "Oh Sacred Head Now Wounded," came across the airwaves, and landed in my heart. I prayed to myself, "*Jesus, your head was wounded so Doug's didn't have to be. Heal him please.*"

Hope Given

Before leaving the hospital, the children and I met with the oncologist, Dr. Ramsdale. She was so kind and told us not to give up hope. "Five to 10 percent of the patients with this kind of brain tumor beat the odds and are alive in 10 years." It was the first good news we had heard. She started

Doug on a promising new oral chemo drug that very day. I was just sure Doug would be in that five to 10 percent. After all, people all over the world were praying for him. We figured there were people in literally each time zone who were praying.

It seemed like an eternity since I received that phone call announcing something was wrong. It's strange how life can throw you a curve, but God still answers prayer. This was one He was sure to answer. Doug was a missionary. He was doing so much good for God. I had no doubt my husband would be the exception.

Chapter 8

THE UPWARD PATH:

To The Courts of the Living God

"Take My Hand Precious Lord and Lead Me Home"

Hymn by George N. Allen, 1844.

"In Sickness and In Health"

Most of us over 40 repeated this vow on our wedding day, giving little thought to the sickness part. I had made a promise. Now I was being called to live it out. How could I possibly do it? It was to be a journey I would later call horrific, yet the greatest privilege I have ever had.

Doug came home from the hospital after being there

for only four days. They say doctors aren't good patients. This was true in Doug's case. He just wanted to be home, even if it was mid- February and the lake was still frozen. It was home!

Our world now consisted of a 1,400 square-foot remodeled cabin on Crooked Lake outside of Petoskey, Michigan. The cabin had a feeling of being very secluded although it was only seven minutes to town. Gone was the excitement of being in the University milieu where we were on the cutting edge of missions. The profound experiences of Albania seemed even further away.

"Doug, how do you feel?" I would ask so I'd know if he needed his pain medicine.

"I feel like I've been in a bar fight at the Elmira Bar with a guy name Rudy and lost."

I guess getting a hole drilled into your head must make you feel like that. (To my knowledge he'd never been in a bar fight!) Depending on how many guys named Rudy hit him – one, two, three, or four, I'd know how bad his head was hurting and would medicate him accordingly.

Two weeks after coming home from the hospital, he started radiation therapy at our local hospital. I wasn't sure he'd go. He knew it probably wouldn't help. I put up a white board in the living room with his daily schedule. This gave him some freedom so he wouldn't continually have to ask what we were doing next. He could just look at the board.

<u>Wednesday April 26th</u>

10 a.m. Nurse Aide here -- bath

12 noon -- Lunch

1 p.m. -- Henry here -- Leave for radiation therapy

6 p.m. -- Dinner

7 p.m. – Rosels' here for dessert

<u>Today's Scripture</u>: "The joy of the Lord is my strength"

Nehemiah 8:10

Friends Forever

Larry Brumfield, a long-time family friend, set up a schedule for helpers to come. At first, it was only overnight. The same person would come every Monday, another person on Tuesday, etc. As his condition deteriorated, people would come at designated times to help me get him up in the chair. Without these wonderful helpers, it wouldn't have been possible for me to keep him in our own bed at home.

I arranged for different friends to come each day, four days a week to take him for treatments. *He'll go with them*, I thought. *He wouldn't give them a hard time.* I would take him on the day we saw the radiologist. This went on for eight weeks. He finally didn't need pain meds. During this time, he had a ball. He was always so social. He loved all who were coming frequently, and he felt he was a much-loved man.

"I just want to go fishing with your dad in Florida," Doug said longingly one day as he looked out at the snow. At the end of his radiation therapy, I took him to Florida. It would be Easter soon. All our children would be coming to Florida to spend it with us.

At the Good Friday service, the pastor asked, "Why me Lord?" during his sermon. I heard Doug sniffle. This obviously resonated within him.

Oh God, you too had to travel a path you didn't want. Strengthen Doug as you did Jesus. Please! Two days later, Easter Sunday, was the last time he went to church. During the service, he needed to go to the bathroom and excused himself. I kept watching for him to come back. He was taking so long. I finally motioned to the usher, a friend of ours, to go look for him.

In a few minutes, he ushered Doug back to his seat. He had forgotten how to get back! It was then I knew we were in trouble. When brain cells die, a part of "who you are" dies as well. My intelligent, educated husband, a natural leader, was reduced to this.

It was spring when we returned to Michigan from Florida. The ice had melted on the lake. Flowers were coming up in the yard. The grass was turning green. New life was everywhere, but in our house.

Since our return, Doug was having a hard time keeping food down. He seemed to be getting more confused. I took him to get another MRI.

"There are some new spots along the mastoid," said the radiologist. "I want to get another opinion." Meanwhile, I took Doug to the Emergency Room where they gave him a liter of I.V. fluid.   He immediately perked up.

The phone was ringing as I walked in the door of the cabin, having just returned from the hospital. The oncologist, Dr. Ramsdale, was on the other end of the line.

"I'm afraid the cancer has spread. I think the best thing to do now is just to keep him comfortable. I'm going to write an order for Hospice to come. Is that okay with you?"

"I... I... guess. Does that mean that we will discontinue the chemo drugs?" I inquired.

"Yes, I'm afraid so. They really aren't helping. I'll call and make the arrangements. I'm so sorry." She hung up the phone while I stood staring at the receiver in my hand.

Hospice came. Doug knew what that meant. It meant there was no hope for a cure. We would now just keep him comfortable. He handled this news as he did everything else in life – with dignity.

The vomiting started again. It was probably from all the accumulated chemo.

"He needs an I.V.," I told the nurse.

"I'm sorry we don't do that," she replied. "Sometimes this is just the body's way of telling us it's time."

I went ballistic. My husband was not ready to die! He just needed fluids from all the vomiting. I went into action. I called a doctor for another opinion. The doctor came to our home and we started an I.V. on Doug. After a few liters of fluid, his mental state was better. He was his old self. He started eating again.

Doug and I had living wills. I was his patient advocate. He had requested that fluids not be withheld. This paper gave me the authority to do what I thought was right. I was a nurse and a strong-willed one at that! More importantly, Doug was the love of my life. He would have the best care possible. I would see to it.

Summer brought the Canadian Geese back to our lake along with white swans, ducks, and a variety of shore birds. The woods next door provided additional cover for deer, rabbits, and raccoons. A mother mallard with her six ducklings paraded her brood across the lawn several times a day to check out any dropping of seeds from the bird feeder.

We watched the ducklings grow throughout the long summer days, which often lasted until almost 11 p.m. The summer flowers were blooming in the yard. The empty lot next door was adorned with multicolored wild flowers. While all this life was happening outside our window, Doug's life was slowly slipping away.

"To Love and To Cherish"

Early on, I had asked God to spare me from watching him die by inches. But now, that is exactly what I was being called upon to do. I also asked God to show me how to love Doug on a "higher level" than only that of a wife.

After his diagnosis, I just hugged him, held him, held his hand and let him weep. I felt I should not put any pressure on him especially as it related to physical love. He was consumed with his own grieving. How could I place demands on him to love me? At this higher level of love, I was being given the privilege of walking through "the valley of the shadow of death" with a man who was a very special person to God. .

Following my prayer, I saw him with new eyes. Without getting into any of the details of his loss of function, I found myself caring for him with the question always before me: *How would I care for him if he were Jesus?*

In the wee hours of the cold morning, when nobody was watching, I'd be tempted to cut corners in his care so I could return to my warm bed. It was at times like that I'd ask myself, *"How would I take care of Jesus?"* Then I'd do the right thing.

Fall had come with shorter days and cooler nights. The maple trees in the yard were turning color. The ducklings were now as large as their parents but still paraded to the feeder each day. As I watched them grow larger, Doug grew weaker.

He was now unable to walk or sit without being propped up. Except for a few hours each day, he was in bed sleeping. Since early June, he was unable to bring his hand to his mouth, so we fed him his meals. He still seemed to know people but talked little, unlike his former sociable self.

It was September 14, our 37th anniversary. Our friends Ralph and Jane Berggren arrived from Washington State. We had celebrated our anniversaries together for the last seven years. They would help me get through this day.

"Doug, today is our anniversary." I told him as I fed him breakfast.

"Really," he responded.   That was his only acknowledgement about this special day. He then forgot.

"Doug, this is the body of Christ given for you," my friend Sam said as we celebrated communion together. I had invited other friends who knew the Berggren's over for dinner. We had gathered around his bed to celebrate communion before going to the dining room for dinner. Doug could not get up by this time. We fed him before we ate.

It was a special time with tears flowing freely for everyone. It would be the last time he had communion. We started our marriage with it. We were now ending our last anniversary with the Lord's presence. We needed Him so…

"Till Death Do Us Part"

It was Friday, October 13, a beautiful warm fall day. Doug had been drifting in and out of consciousness for the last month.

Just this last Sunday, our friend Gary Stevens was in town from Hong Kong to be the mission speaker at our church. He came to visit Doug after church. Gary held his hand and told him, "Doug, you've done a good job. God is so proud of you. It's okay for you to go to Him now." Doug didn't seem to respond, but I believe he heard his words.

The next day, Monday, was the last time he talked to me.

"Oh, Jannie," he sighed.

"What's the matter Doug? Are you tired of it all?" I asked.

He looked at me through tears and just sighed. I crawled into bed next to him and hugged him while rubbing his back. He sighed again. This said it all.

In the late afternoon, our son Matt had arrived with our houseguest Janet. She had been with us that memorable Easter in Albania. It was fitting she was with us now. We sat on the deck looking at the lake and the geese. It was so peaceful, unlike my heart. After Doug's sigh on Monday, I had told God, *"Oh Lord, if You're not going to heal him, would You just take him?"*

Why would I want him to suffer more when the place where he was going would be so glorious?

Doug told me many times before his illness, "I can't wait to see God. I've got lots of questions I want to ask Him." I had a feeling he would be asking Him soon. He was barely conscious. It had gone just as Dr. Ciluffo had said, except I did take care of him at home. It was the way Doug would have wanted it, surrounded by family and friends in his own bed. He now slept most of the time. Today, he knew me. I could tell that by the way he responded when I talked to him.

"How's it going?" Pastor Bill asked as he walked through the front door. We were sitting in the living room while Doug slept in the bedroom.

"I know it's 10:30 [p.m.], but I just got out of a wedding rehearsal. How is he doing?"

"I'm glad you've come," I said. "I'm not sure he's going to make it through the night." After briefing him on Doug's condition, we entered his bedroom.

Pastor Bill climbed up on the bed to face Doug who was lying on his side. "Doug, you've done a wonderful job. The Lord is proud of you. It's okay for you to leave now. You can go to Him. We will carry on. It's okay to leave." He then prayed for God to meet him. After saying his goodbye, Pastor Bill left the bedroom to be with Matt and Janet in the living room.

"Janet, help me turn him over," I yelled to her. As she walked into the bedroom, I continued my assessment, "He's breathing so fast, this might help him breath better." Janet was a Physician's Assistant so she knew how to assist me. The turning didn't help. His fast respirations continued. He seemed very anxious.

"I can't leave him," I said to Janet as I stroked his head. "Please bring me my Bible from the living room."

I read to Doug my devotion for the day.

Psalm 84.

"How lovely is Your dwelling place, O Lord Almighty!

My soul yearns, even faints for the courts of the Lord;

My heart and my flesh cry out

For the living God. . ."

Doug let out a groan.   I continued,

"Even the sparrow has found a home,

And the swallow a nest for her young – a place near Your altar, O Lord Almighty, my King and my God.

Blessed are those who dwell in Your house;

They are ever praising You. . . ."

"A-a-a-h. . . . Ah. . ." he uttered.

"Blessed are those, whose strength is in You,

who set their hearts on pilgrimage.

As they pass through the Valley of Baca (weeping),

They make it a place of springs;

The Autumn rains also cover it with pools."

Just then I noticed the rain hitting the window at the head of his bed.

"Doug, the world is weeping because it is time for you to go." Then I continued. . .

"They go from strength to strength,

Till each appears before God in Zion."

I went back again to reading from the beginning,

My soul yearns, even faints to be in the courts of the Living God."

Another "A-a-a-h. . .ah. . . ."

"My heart and my flesh cry out for the living God."

"A-a-a-h. . . . Ah. . . " Was that his heart and flesh crying out?

His breathing dropped down to around 10 breaths a minute. I turned to Janet and said urgently, "Go get Pastor Bill and Matt in the living room."

Pastor Bill and Matt entered the room with Janet, just as I placed my Bible under Doug's right hand. With my hand over his, I declared, "Doug, you have lived on the "Word". Now it is time for you to go to the "Word." Its okay, you can leave. I'll see you when I get there. It's okay."

"Doug, I'm going to pick up your hand and give it to Jesus. He's going to take it, and take you home." I then picked up Doug's other hand and held it in the air to Jesus. He stopped breathing.

We all looked at one another in amazement. I had actually passed him over to Jesus. What an incredible honor! It was 1:06 a.m. Oct.14, 2000. We all started to praise God, thanking God for Doug's life and for taking him home. We probably stood there for 10 minutes. No crying, just praise. Pastor Bill stood behind Matt and me. He put a hand on each of us and prayed that we would have a double anointing of that which Doug had.

Back in the living room, I put on a tape that I had received earlier that day from my friend Susan Anderson. She had recorded it to be played at Doug's funeral. The beautiful words of Kim Noblitt's song, "If You Could See Me Now," filled the room:

> *Our prayers have all been answered*
> *I finally arrived.*
> *The healing that had been delayed*
> *Has now been realized.*
> *No one's in a hurry, there's no schedule to keep*
> *We're all enjoying Jesus, just sitting at His feet.*
>
> *If you could see me now*
> *I'm walking streets of gold.*
> *If you could see me now*
> *I'm standing tall and whole.*
> *If you could see me now*
> *You'd know I'd seen His face.*
> *If you could see me now*
> *You'd know the pain's erased.*

Doug had passed from sickness to health. My vow was fulfilled. I thought of him being in heaven, and I tried to imagine what he was seeing. We all smiled through our tears, as we thought of what Doug was experiencing as we listened to the words.

It was time to call the family!

Chapter 9

My Path

How will I finish?

Be faithful even to the point of death,

and I will give you the crown of life. (Rev: 2:10)

My Cry to God

"Now it's just me and you God," I spoke aloud, just to make sure He heard me. Sitting in my favorite chair in my cabin, I couldn't avoid it any longer. The past six weeks felt like I was playing a role on the stage of someone else's life. The funeral in Michigan, the memorial service in Hawaii, all seemed like a dream, surreal somehow. The thank you cards were all written, the family returned home, and I was left alone with the painful reality, "He's gone." The finality of it was sinking into my soul – "He's gone."

It was time for a second cup of coffee while I took a second look at my life. My heart was shattered. Like "Humpty Dumpty," it had broken into so many pieces; I didn't see how God could ever put it back together again. I felt so alone; so vulnerable. I was a widow! Me -- a widow!

"This isn't how it was supposed to be Lord," I yelled. "What about me? What now? How do I go on Lord?" I asked between sobs. The thoughts swirled through my mind like a springtime tornado. Doug was not only my husband, but also my best friend. He adored me and lavished attention on me. He told me every morning how beautiful I was, how lucky he was to have me, how much he loved me. When I'd walk into a room, many times he'd stop what he was doing and turn to whoever happened to be there and say, "Doesn't she look beautiful today?" What a man! I smiled at the memory, and then the impact hit me. *Oh Lord, will I ever feel so special again? Who will tell me I'm beautiful?*

Doug and I had worked together as a team after we entered missions, but we each had our own gifting -- they were different but complementary. It reminded me of cross-country skiing; first, one would be out in the front, then the other, just like skis, in perfect rhythm. When the rhythm worked well, we moved forward with great speed and success. He considered me a wise woman and would seek out my counsel on many things, especially after he became Dean of the College of Counseling and Health Care (CCHC). I was half as educated as he was, yet he valued my opinion. *Who would seek my opinion now? Who cared?*

Nothing would ever be the same again. I'd lost more than my husband. My ministry as I knew it was gone as well – it is hard to ski on one ski.

Lord, I cried out, *I want my life to count. I want it to matter that I lived on this earth. I want to make a difference. What do I do now? Will you show me Lord?* I half groaned, not quite audibly. Tears flowed freely. I fell to my knees and sobbed until I was able to whisper, "I want to hear You say to me, 'Well done, good and faithful servant.'"

With a lump in my throat and pain in my heart, I tried to convince myself that my ministry wasn't over just because Doug's was. We had been a team. Now my ministry by necessity would look different. I still have choices to make. Doug's death could become an excuse for me to go back to my secure life before missions. It's easy to find excuses to keep from doing what we know we are called to do. As far as I knew, God hadn't removed the call on my life because He took Doug home. While we were in missions, I felt fully alive. I felt I was doing what I was born for; my life was counting for the Kingdom.

For now, however, I was too exhausted from the care giving of the last eight months and the trauma of losing Doug, to think much about my future. I am a strong person.

When the going gets tough, I just dig in my heels and go on. The loss of my mate humbled me, and I realized I wasn't as strong as I thought! I determined to take a year off, not make any big decisions, and ask God to heal me.

I returned to Kona two and a half months after Doug's death, rented an old Hawaiian-style house on the ocean and just sat and stared at the waves and sunsets. Life can be shorter than we think, and we must not treat it carelessly. I read a few good books to help with my grieving. *My Companion Through Grief: Comfort for Your Darkest Hours* by Gary Kinnaman, helped comfort me. *When Your Soul Aches*, by Lois Mowday Rabey, offered practical suggestions for widows.

Ultimately my thoughts came back to asking, what did my future hold? This would be my consuming question to God over the next months. Many times pain and trouble drive us to consider some of life's deepest questions. I started to ponder: W*hat do I want to do? What do I enjoy doing? What brings me life?*

In his book, *The Dream Maker*, Bruce Wilkinson says, "The minute you decide that you will do whatever it takes, you are already in pursuit of your dream." Are you available for God to use for His purposes? Dr. Wilkinson challenges us to ask ourselves these questions:

- What have I always been good at?
- What do I love to do most?
- What makes me feel most fulfilled?

If we desire to make our life count and earnestly seek God to show us the path, He will! Sometimes we are not willing to pay the price that a change in lifestyle may require so we can live out our deepest desire to serve Him.

If not now, when? The latter may never come! If your desire is to make your life count, God sees your heart and as you pursue Him, He will show you the next step.

The next step. . . hmm. . . . *What do I love to do? – I love seeing and learning new things. What am I good at? – I'm good at organizing things.* I'm a visionary. I love to make a plan and try to implement it. *What makes me feel most fulfilled? – Ministry, seeing God heal people. But I also love taking people on a cross-cultural mission trip and seeing God open their eyes to a greater purpose.* I was always good at organizing, counseling others, and seeing spiritual reality as a visionary.

However, I didn't know until I stepped into a world different from mine that I would find my ultimate fulfillment by exposing others to missions and to the excitement of what God is doing in the world.

What We Leave Behind

Because I was a widow, I didn't have that "special someone" with whom to discuss ideas – Doug and I always talked over important issues. This was a huge loss for me. I was afraid I would make a wrong choice, so I wanted to take it slow. Day after day, as I sat staring at the ocean and pondered my future, I became very pensive. I thought, *"Nuts, just when life was going great, the rules got changed!"* Have you ever had that thought?

My friend, Brad Benbow, asked himself, following Doug's death, "What if I don't have the time left I think? I could be like Doug and die early. How will I stand before the Father if I didn't do what He wanted me to do? I have spent most of my time working in pursuits that have done little to advance the Kingdom of God. What should I change?" Wow! The answer to these questions may very well determine my choices as well.

Midlife is a wonderful time to take stock of where we have been and to regroup and ask ourselves the hard questions. I'm not certain how much time I have left. I need to do NOW whatever God is calling me to do before it is too late.

I must hear God and choose my course wisely; the choices I make not only affect me but others as well. The consequences of my choices have a ripple effect, not only in this life, but for eternity. Many times as Doug and I considered choices set before us, we reasoned, "Why waste energy on things that one year from now will not matter? Wouldn't it be better to invest our time and talents for eternity?"

Invest for eternity – that is what Dr. Derek Chignell is doing. Derek was a chemistry professor at Wheaton

College near Chicago for 26 years. When his wife died, he had a strong conviction that time on this earth is fleeting. He enjoyed teaching but there came a time when he asked himself, "Is this what I want to be doing for the rest of my life? How much time do I have left?" Derek had a gnawing desire to make his life count more for the Kingdom. As he pondered this, a thought dropped into his mind, "*Just use what you know.*" Derek retired early and today, he is using his skills in international missions.

To date, Derek is responsible for nine seminars a year. The seminars are held in the US, Europe, Africa, and Asia. He has two projects going in Central Europe and East Africa. In addition, he has four teams that have started nine water catchments systems, three clinics, and six schools.

By meeting a real need, his team has earned the right to share the Gospel and bring more than just clean drinking water. They bring the ultimate water of life.

What about You?

Have you ever felt God might be calling you to something different; that there might be something more? Are you afraid to answer that call? You too don't how much time you have left. I believe our heart yearns for transcendence. We want to be a part of something bigger than ourselves, outside ourselves. You may say, that's easy for you, you're trained medically, you had something to offer.

Perhaps you are thinking: What do I have to give? I'm just a _____ (*you fill in the blank*).

Can you cook, dig a hole, or play with children? God doesn't just use the educated, *He uses the available*! God told Derek, "Just use what you know."

Have you ever cried out to God as I did, or will you wait for a tragedy before you're brought to your knees? My heart for you the reader is that you will not miss the opportunity to change your course – yes, Midlife if necessary – answer the "call" from God to your very soul.

If you are making excuses, I urge you to stop. God will not ask you to "give up" something without replacing it with something better. We are told by God that we cannot serve both God and money. Could it be that money tests our hearts, our motives, and our character?

Oswald Chambers says in his book, *My Utmost for His Highest,* "Beware of stopping your ears to the call of God . . . when a man begins to overhear that call, then begins agony that is worthy of the name. . . beware of competitors when God does grip you."

In our case, once we let go of the security of a job, we saw God use us in a mighty way. I believe it is a dangerous thing to block your heart from hearing the call of God.

I wonder, what if we had said, *"Not now, later?"* There would be no later for Doug. What if he had waited? Many lives would have been poorer, including mine! We had to move, when we felt the nudge.

Rick Warren states in *The Purpose Driven Life,* "Retirement is not the goal of a surrendered life because it competes with God for the primary attention of our lives. Our primary attention shouldn't be ourselves, but the purposes of God."

Don't wait for retirement to do meaningful things for God. Doug still would not be of retirement age. Doug once made this statement to a friend, "The first half of my life I made a living; the second half, I made a difference!"

All the things we possess are simply "stuff." Doug didn't take anything with him, but he invested in people, those who will spend eternity with the Father. There is a plaque hanging in my cabin which reads:

"One hundred years from now, it won't matter what kind of house I lived in, what kind of car I drove, or what my clothes were like, but what will matter is, I made a difference for eternity!"

I want to live my life worthy of the sacrifice He made. What about you? Can you do any less? What are you giving your time to? Does it have eternal value? Can you tell God, I will serve You no matter what the cost? I know many of you think about mortgages, college and grandkids. I live to testify that if we give those things to Him, He has a way of taking care of our concerns.

The way of the cross sometimes contains times of not

knowing what will happen, times of incomprehensible pain. Jesus asked His closest friends to go through this. Is He asking it of you? If the Spirit is stirring you, tell Him you're available to do whatever He requires of you; then ask Him to direct your paths – He will – just as he did for us and all the amazing people you will read about in the next chapter.

Chapter 10

CHANGED LIVES FROM CHANGED PATHS

The Ripple Effect – Lasting Fruit

"The leaves were used for medicine to heal the nations."

(Revelation 22:2) (NLT)

How can we evaluate the significance of our lives? Is this measured in money, property, or awards? No, the measure of a life is determined by the ruler of the Universe. Nothing else we do will matter as much as helping people find an eternal relationship with God. We should all consider ourselves missionaries working undercover as plumbers, teachers, bank tellers, bus drivers, secretaries and so on.

Eric Liddell said in the movie, *Chariots of Fire*, "When I run I feel His pleasure." I believe that is the key! Doing God's will causes us to be satisfied with our life when we know we are walking *His path*.

Most people would consider Doug a success by any standard. However, in his own eyes, when he moved from his everyday work world to embrace the world of missions, he moved from "success to significance."

Fruit from His Leadership

Doug's decision to obey the voice of God had lasting ramifications all over the world. He sought to develop – and multiply – training programs according to the needs in the field.   Making the decision to become Dean of the College of Counseling and Health Care (CCHC) was difficult, but consider the fruit it bore.

Kit Ying: Helping the Least of These

Kit Ying, a young woman in our mission, was horrified to discover the dying rooms in the state-run orphanage in China where she worked. The children -- mostly girls or handicapped boys -- were left to die in rooms where they were not given any care. They lay in wet, dirty diapers and were not held or fed. Workers reasoned that since they were dying anyway, it would be a waste of baby formula to feed them.

One day Kit Ying asked permission to take a little girl home with her. She bathed her, put clean diapers on her, cuddled her and took her to bed with her. Within a few days, the child started to respond. Then Kit Ying had an inspired idea. What if she found foster homes that would take in these children and care for them just as she was doing in her home? They could be part of a family.

For children who couldn't be placed into foster homes, Mother's Choice and Mother's Love orphanages were born. The concept of valuing the child as God values the child was so foreign that it soon became apparent that workers would need to be trained to care for these children and to minister the love of God to them.

Enter Doug Kinne with a heart overflowing with love for the at-risk children of the world. He was convinced that Satan particularly targeted women and children, and this troubled him deeply. The memory of the street child in Guyana from our first mission's trip haunted him. *What was being done to help these children?* If you engaged Doug in a conversation about it, he'd get teary-eyed or angry. It was clear that God had given him His passion for hurting children and those nobody wanted.

Doug and Kit Ying met with Gary Stephens, then a member of YWAM's Global Leadership Team, and Carol Boyd, then International Dean of the College of Education. One afternoon in 1999, the three of them sat down in Carol's living room to seek God concerning these children. Out of their prayers and discussion was birthed the Introduction to

Children's Social Service (ICSS) School.

The goal of ICSS is to train workers to minister to the disenfranchised children of the world, such as the handicapped, orphans, and street children. God had put on each of their hearts a portion of His heart for these children. Gary and Kit Ying recognized the "skill gaps" they saw in the two orphanages. They also saw a need to impart the value of the child to the caregivers, especially as it related to the institutionalized child. God was showing them He cared deeply for all His children wherever they lived.

After Doug's death, YWAM changed the school name to "Children at Risk." This course is held in Costa Rica, Rwanda, and each year in Burtigny, Switzerland. A shorter version is held as a seminar to accommodate those who are working full time and cannot drop out of their ministries for nine months. Some of those involved early on were people such as Janna Moats, who started "The Women and Children's Advocacy Centre." The (WCAC) provides networking, resources and gives training for people helping with vulnerable women and children. The focus is on connecting, supporting and mobilizing through creating awareness of the global issues.

Julie Sitz, a young woman Doug had encouraged to take the ICSS class, went on to get her BA in Children's Social Services. She helped train others in Cambodia and Switzerland. Eva Spangler, an artist and teacher, shared with me that Doug and this class has influenced her work. She continues to be involved with helping children. To date, this work is continuing in Africa, China, India, Brazil, and

Cambodia. - The ripple continues.

China: Lin Yi Helps the Handicapped

Lin Yi accompanied Doug as his translator on a fact-finding trip to mainland China. A young man in his twenties, Lin Yi had completed a YWAM school in Okinawa, where he met his Japanese wife, Hiromi Hashii.

One night at dinner, Lin Yi shared his vision to start a school for handicapped children in his home province in China. He had been given some land from the government and even had a name picked out, but didn't know how to start a school.

Doug helped him find the funds to take the ICSS class. After completing his training, Lin Yi started a school in China in 2000 with 23 deaf students and one Down Syndrome student. Every year the number of students he is able to help is growing. I was invited to attend the dedication of the new school and hospital he built on land given him.. Lin Yi is a good investment. I have no doubt he will continue to find ways to help many more people He is another example of the ripple effect of the obedience of one couple to leave the security of a paycheck and step out into the unknown world of listening to the voice of God and doing what He asks. God said obedience is better then sacrifice. I believe when we obey what we know and do what we know, God does the rest.

HIV/AIDS: Penny's Story

The HIV/AIDS situation had long been on Doug's heart. *"What an opportunity for the church. This is the hour to respond,"* Doug said many times. He knew there were whole villages in Africa that are mostly children because the adults have died of AIDS.

The desperate need was confirmed when he asked Steve Goode, YWAM's Director of Mercy Ministries, what he needed most on the field.

Steve's reply was direct: "Send me a thousand HIV/AIDS workers."

About that time, Penny Dugan's world was falling apart. Her life had seemed to be practically perfect until the day her husband Ted announced he was a homosexual and left her and their three children to live with his male lover.

Ted suggested that they both get tested for HIV/AIDS. Penny's results came back negative but Ted's was positive. This, plus the fact Ted would not give up his lover, made them choose divorce. Ted preferred to live with his lover. Penny and her children came to the University of the Nations in Kona, Hawaii, for three months to take a class and get away from the situation. When they returned to Kansas, they learned that Ted was dying of AIDS.

Although she said it was the hardest thing she ever had to do, Penny took care of Ted until he died, working daily alongside his lover. She and Ted had a great friendship, and he dearly loved his kids. Before he died, he called them all in for a talk. He told them how sorry he was and that he loved them. In the end, Penny's love had extended Christ's love to Ted.

This beautiful act of loving care-giving was the beginning of a ministry. After Ted died, Penny saw there were other HIV/AIDS patients who had no one to care for them at the end of their lives. Penny was not a nurse. She had no special training but she started a group home for those who had nowhere to go to die in dignity. Many saw her love and received Christ before they died.

When Penny recounted her story to Doug, he was deeply moved. This prompted him to explore the possibility of training workers to help care for those nobody wanted, those with HIV/AIDS.

Doug knew the average person is not educated concerning the facts of HIV/AIDS. Such ignorance may cause fear and suspicion and prevent others from becoming involved. At the time, few knew how to minister to HIV/AIDS patients and their families.

By the time most people in developing nations receive a diagnosis of HIV/AIDS, they are usually months away from death. Most will slip into eternity without knowing the forgiveness or the love of our Savior. Both Doug and Steve recognized the need to train people for this ministry and the urgent need arising from this pandemic.

Doug counseled with Penny and with Carla van der Kooij, a Dutch lady who had started a school for children affected with HIV/AIDS in Belo Horizonte, Brazil. The three of them crafted a course for the U of N to train HIV/AIDS workers. Doug selected Sue Green, an RN, to lead the first class in Kona. Doug never saw this vision come to fruition; he died before the first class started..

Nevertheless, God picked strategic people for this first class. Oby and Kanayo are emerging leaders in Nigeria, and Diganta runs a micro enterprise industry for former prostitutes and an HIV/AIDS ministry in Calcutta.

Today, the HIV/AIDS class is held somewhere in the world each quarter. A more compact four-week seminar on this topic is also being offered, training missionaries going to other countries as well as HIV/AIDS workers for the developed world. School leaders also hope to duplicate the class in Africa where the need is so acute. Penny has moved almost full time to Africa and is running a center for those infected with the disease They plan to go to strategic parts of the world offering a shorten version as a seminar to train indigenous people to be HIV/AIDS trainers. This will cause a ripple effect, trainers who train trainers, thus getting the information to those who most need it.

What is the measure of a man's obedience? We never know the impact our obedience will have on a whole segment of society. I believe God is pleased with Penny's obedience and Doug's obedience.

Fruit from Guyana

Robin Mclean, our driver in Guyana, called to say he was moving to the US. He asked Doug to disciple him. We invited him to come live with us. For the next two years we watched him grow in his faith. He eventually moved to New Jersey to be near his mother who had also immigrated. Today, he is married to Kim, and lives with his 14-year-old daughter. He works at the Christian school his daughter attends and frequently sings solos in his church, using what he has to glorify God.

Fruit from Albania

Our translators Luli and Patroit are continuing to make a difference. Luli rose to the post of Nursing Coordinator for the nation of Albania. She has since moved to Canada.

Patroit is married with two children. He led his wife to the Lord, moved to the village of Korca where he started a church and a medical clinic. He is passionate for the Lord. They are effectively helping to disciple a nation.

Fruit from Ukraine

Craig Wendt, his wife Pat, and family returned home after their outreach to the Carpathian Mountains in Ukraine. He spoke with the Chaplin of the local hospital about taking teams from the hospital in Michigan back to run clinics among the Gypsies. Dave Behling, then the Chaplin, began leading two short-term medical missions' trips each year. Another Crossroads DTS class from Kona continued to go back yearly. This has multiplied to see the establishment of five churches, two medical clinics and a well with clean drinking water for one of the villages. Lives are changed, people are receiving medical care, and the Gospel is being proclaimed!

Paul Hurley was an undertaker before becoming one of our students. We put him on the medical team because he knew the human body well. By helping us in the clinic, he developed a love for the people. Paul and his wife, Gayla, returned to Ternopil, Ukraine and have lived there for the last ten years. They run a soup kitchen for the poor, a medical clinic using local physicians, and have a vitamin distribution program for the children. Gayla also leads Bible studies in their home.

One of the children who went with her parents to the Ukraine in 1994 was Stacy Orrico. She is a well known as a national recording artist and has appeared on The Today Show and numerous other programs. Her parents took our class, and took her on an overseas outreach – did those events have an impact on her? I would like to think so. Today her mission field has expanded to include the youth of our country.

Fruit That Can't Be Measured

If you were to talk with any of the 400 or so Midlife

students we helped train, they would all have a story to tell about how Doug and the programs changed them. Then there are all the students and staff in the healthcare schools, plus all the ministries our students have started worldwide. Doug estimated he delivered about 6,000 babies in his medical career, but how many spiritual babies did he touch for the Kingdom? Only heaven knows!

This is what really matters. Doug finished the task given him to do! He heard the call, he completed the task. Now it is my turn with what time I have left. What could I possibly consider in this life to be more important, than when I stand before the Father, to hear Him say to ME, "Well done good and faithful servant, you finished the task given you to do."

A Poignant Moment

It was a perfect spring day, the sky a clear blue. It was 74 degrees, and the lilacs were spectacular as were all the spring blossoms on the trees. The dark blue of Lake Michigan was visible off in the distance. *This is such a peaceful, beautiful place,* I thought.

It was only hours ago that I stood at the church. My daughter, our youngest, was about to be married to Doug Piper. Neither of us wanted to spoil the day so we didn't say what we both had heavy on our hearts. Our eyes met and locked. A knowing look passed between us. Tears welled up in my eyes. She looked away to avoid tears, not wanting anything to ruin her makeup. She looked so lovely, so happy. No, we didn't want anything to spoil this happy day! As the music started, Tamara walked down the aisle on the arm of her oldest brother Rex and into a new life with her husband.

Following the reception, I stood with my parents, my two sons, and Doug's sister, Joan. We had another mission. My daughter and her new husband were off on their honeymoon. Before they left, she handed me her bridal bouquet. "Take it with you," she said, knowing our destination.

So, on this beautiful warm spring day, here we were. Large towering white pine trees stood high above us. Under them the beautiful, large black stone stood stately in front of us. It reads:

KINNE
Dr. Douglas
Nov. 1, 1941 - Oct.14, 2000
He finished the task given him to do (Acts 20:24)

We all stood in hushed silence. Then I knelt down at my husband's grave and placed our daughter's bridal bouquet on it. Time seemed to hang in space. No one said a word. Shortly, I heard a few sniffles behind me. I got up. It was time to leave — time to leave the past and walk into my new life. After all — it was spring — my path continues. I want to be known as a finisher too — one who finished well.

Postscript

Eight and a half years have passed since Doug's home going. It hasn't always been easy living my life without him, but God has been faithful to meet all my needs. Since Doug's Death, our family has increased. Our daughter Tamara married a wonderful man also named Doug. I now have my grand daughter Brianna and twin grandsons. I still serve with YWAM at the University of the Nations in Kona, Hawaii. I'm a nurse, not an English major; yet during this time of reflection, I sensed God seemed to be saying, *"Tell others your story, and write a book."* Writing this book has opened up a whole new world of people and adventures.

On February 19, 2006, I married author, Jim Conway. Jim is also a Speaker and former pastor. This is another change in direction for me, one that is unfamiliar and at times scary. I find myself speaking at conferences and on radio programs. I need to trust God now in this new direction just like I did in the past. God has been faithful to me both married and single. Now, I may speak to millions, but my heartbeat is for the lost. I believe I will remain involved in missions in some way until God calls me home. This is the path I have been called to walk. This is the walk I hope to finish.

Study Guide

With the explosion of the information age, world unrest, and the growing chasm between the rich and poor, this might be a good time for reflection. "What are my l long term goals, and how am I going to use the rest of my life to make a difference?"

To look back on our life and say "Is this all there is?" Or ask ourselves, "Is this what I want to be doing for the rest of my life?" For some of us the answer is "yes," but for others as we reflect on where we've been and where we are going, we may sense that what we thought would bring us happiness hasn't quite satisfied.

Perhaps you're in midlife or have recently been downsized. Is God calling you to something new, or reminding you of a desire He has already put in your heart of something He would have you to do? The following questions are presented for those who might want to consider a change in direction or emphasis. They can be pondered individually, with your spouse, or in a discussion group.

If you choose to do the latter, you might want to consider reading a chapter a week, go through the "Points to Ponder" and "Practical Steps to Proceed," and then, for the first six weeks, read and discuss one of the stories from Chapter 10. The "Prayer for Pruning" is a suggested way to close, but my prayer is that God's heart will speak to your heart for your life direction.

Chapter 1

A HETIC PATH: *Life is too Busy*

Points to Ponder:

1. What is it you have always felt God calling you to do?

2. Do you have a nagging feeling you haven't completed it yet?

3. What circumstances would cause you to want to make a life change?

Practical Steps to Proceed:

1. Inquire about the possibility of taking a sabbatical or leave of absence from your work.

2. Find out if you qualify for some time off, or what it would take to qualify.

3. Ask your pastor, friends, or missionaries you know about short-term mission opportunities

Prayer for Pruning:

Dear God, sometimes I feel as if I'm stuck in the rat race. The only race I want to be in is your race. Help me not to wait for *someday,* but to say "yes" to You now. Amen.

Chapter 2

A NEW PATH: *Trying out a New Lifestyle*

Points to Ponder:

1. What is your passion? What drives you?

2. Has God ever broken your heart for the things that break His?

3. What breaks His Heart?

Practical Steps to Proceed:

1. Take a short-term missions trip to see how you function cross-culturally or volunteer at a local homeless or food shelter.

2. Discuss with your spouse or a good friend various options God may be placing before you.

3. Make a one month, one year, and five year goal for your life.

Prayer for Pruning:

God, break my heart for the things that break your heart. Show me how I can bring Your Love into these situations. Amen.

Chapter 3

EARLY LIFE PATH:
Birth, School, Marriage and Family

Points to Ponder:

1. Is there a traumatic event in your past that has changed your future?

2. How does the religious training of your childhood speak to you today?

3. How has God been directing your paths through the early seasons of your life?

Practical Steps to Proceed:

1. Share family photos with your children and recall the faithfulness of God.

2. Craft a legacy to leave for your family (write a short story, a poem, or a book; create a photo album; make a piece of furniture, etc.)

3. Set up a college fund for your children. Ask the Lord for wisdom on how to do this.

Prayer for Pruning:

Lord, use my circumstances if necessary to change my life's direction if You want me to be following a different path than the one I am on. Amen.

Chapter 4

PREPARING FOR A NEW LIFE PATH:
Skill Development

Points to Ponder:

1. What is the difference between "making a difference" and "making a living?"

2. What would it take for you to make a difference, in addition to making a living?

3. Are you prepared to be flexible when your expectations aren't met?

Practical Steps to Proceed:

1. Define the obstacles to overcome before you can make a career change.

2. Investigate options for overcoming them, i.e., paying down the mortgage, scholarship for college, etc.

3. Set a timeline for completing these goals.

Prayer for Pruning:

Father, it is hard for me to see how it might be possible for me to make a change in my life. If this is Your will for me, make a way where I see no way. Amen.

Chapter 5

UNCHARTED PATH:
Opening a Closed Country

Points to Ponder:

1. Do you know or have a hunch about something new God may be calling you to?

2. How could you use your life skills to make a difference?

3. What decision have you always been happy you made? What unhappy decisions did you make?

Practical Steps to Proceed:

1. Look at one of the websites listed under the **Resources** section of this book.

2. Ask God to give you a heart for a country or a people group.

3. Do some research on that country or people group.

Prayer for Pruning:

Oh God, let us not fear leaving our own paradise to take the good news of Jesus to the hard places of this world. Amen.

Chapter 6

TRAVELING OUR NEW PATH:

Comfortable in Our Calling

Points to Ponder:

1. What talent or skill could you use for God?

2. What is keeping you from using it for Kingdom work?

3. If you knew what God wanted you to do, would you abandon your agenda for God's agenda?

Practical Steps to Proceed

1. Work out your retirement plan now.

2. Plan your investments so you have liquidity.

3. Start giving away things you no longer use.

Prayer for Pruning

Lord, I want to use my talents and skills for Your kingdom. Would you please show me how? In faith, I give You my future. Amen.

Chapter 7

ROCKS IN THE PATH:

Our Greatest Challenge

Points to Ponder:

1. Discuss how you would feel if you were given a terminal diagnosis.

2. What, if any, changes would you make?

3. What is keeping you from making those changes now?

Practical Steps to Proceed:

1. Make out a will if you haven't. Include power of attorney for medical decisions.

2. Discuss this with your family.

3. Write each member in your family a letter telling them what they mean to you. Seal it and put it in a safe place to be read following your death.

Prayer for Pruning:

Lord, help me to relate to those I love today as if this were my last day. Show me if there is any thing I need to "make right." Let me live each day as a gift from You. Amen

Chapter 8

THE UPWARD PATH:

To the Courts of the Living God

Points to Ponder:

1. If today were my last, am I ready to stand before the Father?

2. How can I make the remainder of my life count more than it has?

3. Will I have any regrets? If so, what?

Practical Steps to Proceed:

1. Make a list of important information others will need to know on your death, i.e., insurance policy, where you keep important papers such as your will, etc.

2. Buy a cemetery plot or discuss cremation possibilities with your family. Consider ordering the headstone and have it placed. It's one less thing for the family to deal with!

3. Plan your funeral and write your wishes, including favorite scriptures and songs. Tell someone where to find this information.

Prayer for Pruning:

Father, let my life purpose be Your purpose for me. Let me hear when I stand before you, "Well done." Amen.

Chapter 9

MY PATH:

How will I Finish?

Points to Ponder:

1. What difference will it make that I ever lived?

2. What can I leave beyond the grave?

3. Will I hear the Father say, "Well done, good and faithful servant?

Practical Steps to Proceed:

1. Arrange to leave a portion of your assets to your church, a mission organization or favorite charity.

2. Invest time in a child, especially passing on to them your faith.

3. Spend time alone with God asking Him how this book relates to your life situation.

Prayer for Pruning:

Lord, I want to be like Jesus, I want to seek to do the will of the Father. I give my future into Your hands. Amen.

Chapter 10

CHANGED LIVES

The Ripple Effect

Points to Ponder:

1. Identify ripple effects from your life.

2. Can your legacy be passed on?

3. Are you satisfied with your ripple at this point in your life?

Practical Steps to Proceed:

1. Verbally encourage someone everyday. (ie. children, bank tellers, grocery clerks, etc.)

2. Look for needs that you can meet.

3. Get involved — Bible study, homeless, short term mission trip.

Prayer for Pruning:

Father, I want to leave a legacy that has lasting value. Show me the path that leads to making a difference. Amen.

Do You Need A Personal Connection With God?

Doug would want me to include this section in the book. It was his passion that others know his Savior. He wants to spend eternity with you!

If you have accepted Jesus Christ as your personal Savior, you **will** spend eternity with God and with Doug.

Jim Becks is a friend who shared with me he knew all about Jesus, but never knew it was possible to have a personal relationship with him. He accepted Christ as his personal Lord and Savior and so can you!

Please pray this prayer from your heart:

Lord Jesus, I confess to you that I am a sinner. Forgive me of all my sins. I believe that you died on the cross for my sins, rose again and now live in Heaven. I accept you as my Lord and Savior, and I ask you to come live in my heart. Teach me your ways, that I may be more like you. Amen.

For those of you who prayed this prayer for the first time, I would suggest you start reading the Bible. The Gospel of John in the New Testament is a good place to start. Find a church that believes the Bible is the inspired Word of God. It might also be helpful to find a small group of friends to pray with and study the Bible together.

If you prayed this prayer for the first time, would you let me know? Go to our website, www.midlife.com, and contact us. I would be so blessed to know that Doug's message is still going on and bearing fruit for God's Kingdom.

Dr. Douglas Kinne 1941-2000

"Well Done, Good and Faithful Servant!"

RESOURCES

Websites

www.thefinishers.org – A complete website that matches midlife baby boomers to appropriate ministries with great links to other ministries and organizations. The Finisher's Forum holds several meetings each year for networking, information gathering and missionary preparation.

www.servantopportunities.net – This site also links ministry-minded persons with opportunities to serve God.

www.uofnkona.edu – Doug and Jan trained and served at the University of the Nations in Kona, Hawaii. This site gives details on the five-month Discipleship Training School (DTS), and Crossroads Discipleship Training School (CDTS).

www.intercristo.com – This site offers full-time opportunities for service in your area of expertise.

www.worldconcern.org – Offers opportunities to practice medicine worldwide on a short-term basis.

www.healthteamsintl.org – Offers short term mission opportunities for physicians, dentists, nurses, dental hygienist.

www.swi.net – Strategic World Impact assists the church in developing a strategy for the harvest through providing food, medicine and spiritual resources.

www.midlife.com – Insights for dealing with the confusion and stress often associated with the Midlife transition. This is my website.

www.gmojoinus.com – A new and very exciting approach to evangelism: Bringing people to Jesus internationally, via the internet, from your home.

**Intermedia
Publishing Group**

Publishing That Works For You

Do you need a speaker?

Do you want Jan Kinne Conway to speak to your group or event? Contact Larry Davis at: (623) 337-8710, or email: ldavis@intermediapr.com or use the contact form at: www.intermediapr.com or www.midlife.com.

To purchase bulk copies of *The Finisher* or buy another book for a friend, get it at: www.imprbooks.com or at my website www.midlife.com.

Terry, our Publisher/Editor, has been great to work with. If you have a book you would like to publish, contact Terry Whalin, Publisher, at Intermedia Publishing Group, (623) 337-8710 or email: twhalin@intermediapub.com or use the contact form at: www.intermediapub.com.